MY EXPERIENCES IN A LUNATIC ASYLUM

BY A SANE PATIENT

by Herman Charles Merivale

'Let us rise and revolt against those people, Lankin. Let us war with them and smite them utterly. It is to use against these, especially, that scorn and satire were invented'

'And the animal you attack,' says Lankin, 'is provided with a hide to defend him—it is a common ordinance of nature'—M. A. Titmarsh

Originally published in 1879.

I.

It's a mad world, my masters.

I suppose that the motto I have affixed to the first chapter of the brief history of a singular personal experience is by this time an accepted axiom. Was it in one of Mr. Sala's columns of gossip that I was reading the other day of the man of the pen who commented upon the imprisonment in an asylum of a brother of his craft merely by saying, 'What a fool he must be! For years I have been as mad as he, only I took care never to say so'? There are odd corners in the brains of most of us, filled with queer fancies which are as well kept out of sight; eccentricities, I suppose they may be called. The man who is so 'concentric' as to be innocent of peculiarities is a companion of a dull sort. But Heaven help us all when such things may be called, and treated as, madness. For, if all of us were used according to our deserts in that way, who should escape the modern substitutes for whipping? England would not contain the asylums that should be constructed, and might go far to deserve the Gravedigger's description of her for Hamlet's benefit: 'There the men are as mad as he.' Let me go a step further. There are few of us, perhaps, who have not seen something in our lives of the strange nervous disorders which have been generalised as 'hypochondria,' which are, in fact, I think, the different outcomes of a common affection—temporary exhaustion of brain. Beyond a certain point it becomes delirium, the wandering of weakness which is so closely connected with many forms of illness, both in the beginning and during the course and recovery. When the victims of delirium may be added to the eccentric members of society; when at any moment the certificates of any two doctors who may be utter strangers to the patient—

acting under the instructions of friends who are frightened and perplexed, perhaps, and try to believe that they are 'doing for the best' (I leave out of consideration here the baser motives which, it is to be feared, come sometimes into play)—may condemn him to the worst form of false imprisonment, the death-in-life of a lunatic asylum, at a time when he is himself practically unconscious;—who is there amongst us who can for a moment believe himself safe? Death-in-life did I say? It is worse; for it is a life-in-life, worse than any conceivable form of death. The sights and sounds through which one has to live can never be forgotten by him who has lived through them, but will haunt him ever and always. Never let next friends persuade themselves that they are 'doing for the best' for him for whom they so do. For themselves they may think that they are. For him they cannot possibly do worse. Every nerve should be strained to save a man from that fate, if it be humanly possible, ay, even if he be mad indeed; for while there is life there is hope, till that step has been taken. When it has, I verily believe that hope is reduced to its smallest. For the personal experience which I have to tell has taught me this: that the man who comes sane and safe out of the hands of mad-doctors and warders, with all the wonderful network of complications which, by Commissioners, certificates, and Heaven knows what, our law has woven round the unlucky victim in the worst of all its various aberrations, is very sane indeed. And very safe too, happily. His lines afterwards are not altogether pleasant. The curious looks and whispers, the first meetings with old friends, the general anxiety that he should not 'excite himself' (which he may be better excused for doing than most people, perhaps), magnified, no doubt, by his own natural sensitiveness, are difficult in their way. He does not mind them much, is amused by them at times; for, with the strong sense of right on one's side, conflict is rather pleasant than not to the well-balanced soul. But the thread of life and work and duty has been rudely broken by the shock, and has to be knit again under great drawbacks. It can be done, though; and one starts again the wiser and the better man.

'Jurant, quoiqu'un peu tard, qu'on ne l'y prendra plus.' It is no bad thing to have part of one's work and duty so clearly pointed out as this of mine. When this evil question is being stirred to its depths as it is now, every contribution of personal experience is valuable. It is not for me to suggest schemes of reform, as it is the fashion to ask critics to do, but for those who are paid to do that work rightly and earnestly, or who choose to undertake to legislate for us. Nor have I any advice to offer them except the advice of Hamlet: 'O, reform it altogether.' The system is radically wrong, all through, under which such wrong is possible. And I believe it all the more because it seems to me without reasonable excuse. Madness is the most terrible of all visitations; but also, probably for that very reason, the most unmistakable. And in spite of doctors and lawyers and the whole artillery of organised Humbug, I have deduced another lesson from this hard experience of mine: I do not believe that there is any mistaking a madman when you see him.

The especial experience which I have to tell has nothing especially painful, and is, perhaps, none the worse for that. I have nothing to write of dark rooms or strait-waistcoats or whippings, or to reveal such secrets of the prison-house as will make each particular hair to stand on end by the telling. My lines were cast in pleasant places. The private asylum in which I was confined for many months, which in the retrospect seem like one dreary dream, is, I believe, highly recommended by Her Majesty's Commissioners as a delightful sanitary resort—quite a place to spend 'a happy life.' During those months I had the advantage of living in a castellated mansion, in one of the prettiest parts of England, which I shall hate to my dying day, with a constant variety of attendants, who honoured me by sleeping in my room, sometimes as many as three at a time. I was dying in delirium and prostration, simply, and wasted to a shadow; consequently voted 'violent,' as the best way out of it. With carriages to take me out for drives, closed upon wet days, open on fine; with cricket and bowls and archery for the summer, and a pack of harriers to follow across country in the winter; with the head of the establishment, who lived in a sweet little cottage with his family, to give me five o'clock tea on the Sundays; with five refections a day whereof to partake, with my fellow-lunatics, if so disposed, in my private sitting-room when I could not stand it; with a private chapel for morning prayers or Sunday service, the same companions and attendants for a congregation, and some visitors who would come to look at us; with little evening parties for whist or music amongst 'ourselves,' and a casual conjuror or entertainer from town to distract us sometimes for an evening; with an occasional relative to come and see me, beg me not to get excited, and depart as soon as possible,— what more could man desire? As I look at this last sentence of mine it reads like an advertisement. Stay—I had forgotten the medicine. They did not give me very much of it, I suppose, or I should not be alive. Indeed, it seemed to me that the general principle was to give it when one asked for it, and pretty much what one asked for. When I got unusually weak and delirious a good strong dose on the 'violent' theory—homœopathy, I suppose, from a new point of view—was enough, literally, to reduce me to reason. For then I became too weak to speak, and the matter ended for a time.

All this bears so fair an outside that it seems difficult to quarrel with it. Yet the life that it concealed was inconceivably terrible. My head was full of the weakest, the most varying, the most wandering fancies—the fancies of sheer and long-continued exhaustion. These parties, games, entertainments, meals, without a friend's face near me, without hope, wish, or volition; with the shouts and cries of the really violent to wake me sometimes at night; with every form of personal affliction to haunt and mock and yet companion me by day; with poor fellows playing all sorts of strange antics round me, herded together anyhow or nohow, with or without private rooms of their own—more, I am afraid, in proportion as their friends could or would pay for them or not, on the footing of 'first-class patients' than on any other intelligible principle; with Death in the house every now and then, falling suddenly and terribly on one of these unhappy outcasts from some unsuspected malady within, which they could not explain, spoken of in whispers, and hushed up and forgotten as soon as might be; with the warders—'attendants,' if you like it better— playing their rough horse-play all over the great house, the Philistines making sport of the poor helpless Samsons, and varying their amusements by coarse and gross language which made the chilled blood run colder;—the story makes me shrink in the telling, and almost regret that I have undertaken to tell it.

But the evil wants cautery to the very core, and I believe that every story of the kind should be told. To me personally death was very near indeed in that house more than once, from the most complete and absolute exhaustion of brain. I felt it at the time as I have known it since. Death in utter solitude, save for the warders by my side, whose duty it was—or they interpreted it as such, some of them— to hold me down and jump upon me, or kneel on my breastbone, if I turned round or uttered any wandering words in bed. When I was really dying, happily, I was too weak for movement or for word. And there is no stranger comment on the strange nature of the great and common mystery than the fact that in those supreme moments, unconscious of all else, I felt consciously and intensely happy—happier than I have ever felt, perhaps, in all my life. But I had to live, and I did. And so sound was the brain in all its weakness that I have hardly forgotten a single detail of my life in that place, scarcely even any of the vague and wandering fancies that possessed the starved head; so vague and wandering that, had I told one-fourth of them to the doctor, to whom I told (on the principle of Mr. Sala's friends) far too many, all Bedlam itself had not been held more mad than I. What I call fancies they call 'delusions.' And as such I believe that they are written in the Book of the Chronicles of the Commissioners of Lunacy. For we know with what parental care these shameful things are done.

Mr. Dillwyn and others have been doing their best of late to stir the public mind upon this matter, and some recent reports in the newspapers may have materially helped them. But the Home Secretary, I see, has gracefully deferred enquiry to the more convenient season which, from the time of Felix downwards, has been found difficult to secure again. It is easier, probably, to make a great flourish of fireworks in the way of foreign politics,—and with much blowing of the trumpet to restore Great Britain to her former post among the nations, which some of us never could see how or when she had forfeited; and the very deference paid her in this Cyprian business seems to show that she had not,—than to deal with a home-problem like this, which falls so fatally within the province of our old friend the Circumlocution Office, and involves so great a variety of 'British interests' of a peculiar and individual kind. Interests, did I say? Indeed it does, for it involves the liberties and lives of every one of us. It is all very well to plume ourselves upon our charters and our immunities, and to bless those Northern stars of ours that we are not as other men are. But the case of Vera Vasilovitch (if that was her name), over which we jubilated so much at the expense of the benighted Russians, implies no greater danger than these evil lunacy laws. Once in their grasp it is a hard matter, indeed to get out of it. Cowards at the best, all of us, we are all of us afraid of the very name of 'madness' more than of anything else; and in that fear lies the security of the present system against any attack that may be made upon it.

There was a story the other day in an American newspaper of a lady who was spirited away by two scoundrels under the eyes of a whole party of travellers, not one of whom raised a finger to protect her when the fellows had whispered it about that she was 'mad.' This story may not have been true; but it was so singularly ben trovato that it very well may have been; and the mere possibility of its truth argues the necessity of keeping our eyes well open to the dangers in which we live. I suppose that we most of us rather laughed at Charles Reade's attack upon private asylums, and quietly comforted ourselves with the reflection that 'in the nineteenth century' (an expression which is used as a sort of talisman, apparently, like the 'Briton' of Palmerston's day) such things are impossible. It requires a personal experience of their amenities, such as fell to my lot, seriously to believe that the adventures of a novel may be transferred to the pages of an 'article,' and be as strange—and true. Villainous conspiracies, for personal motives, to set the lunacy law in motion, are rare enough, I do not doubt. But the law favours them. What is not rare, I

doubt even less, is the imprisonment in these fearful places
of people who are perfectly sane, but suffering from some
temporary disorder of the brain, the most delicate and
intricate part of all the mechanism, and the least
understood; and if asylums are a sad necessity for the really
mad,—and even that I cannot help doubting; for from what
I have seen I believe that they require a much more loving
and more direct personal supervision than they can get,
poor people,—for the nervous sufferers who are not mad
they are terrible. The mad folk seemed to me happy enough
on the whole, perhaps. But the suffering of those conscious
of being sound of mind, but very sick in body, yet treated
as sound of body and sick in mind—the life of the same
among the mad, baffles description. They must be driven
mad there by the score. I know what it is for men; what
must it be for women? Personally, I do not believe I could
have borne another week of it, for heart and brain were
strained almost to bursting. What would have happened to
me I do not know, for I had lost all care for anything. Nor
did the kindly doctor, under whose advice I was saved, 'in
spite of fortune,' ay, and in spite of myself, pretend to
know either. But he believes that I must have broken down
utterly, probably from softening of the brain.

Sitting at my desk as I am sitting now, with the comforting
pipe and jug of beer by my side (deadly poisons to me, both
of them, I have been often assured), and with a profound
and grateful sense of extreme physical wellbeing, it is
difficult for me to believe that not so long ago I was
pronounced to be suffering at different times or all at once
from epilepsy, partial paralysis, fits, delusions, suicidal and
homicidal mania, 'voices' (a very professional and
dangerous piece of humbug, of which I shall have more to
say presently), 'visions' (Anglicè, dreams), and the Lord
knows what beside. As I was utterly prostrate from

weakness, it reads like a dangerous complication; and I feel with pride that I may safely challenge Maria Jolly herself to the proof. It is something to have lived through all these maladies, and to be engaged in replenishing the welcome beer-glass, or, like the moralist of Thackeravian memory,

Alive and merry at—year,

Dipping my nose in the Gascon wine.

But it is not too much to say,—and I speak again the wise words of my good friend and doctor, not my own,—that there are at this present moment languishing in these places many men who might well have been rescued, may be even now (and a mob attack, Bastille fashion, upon the whole body of private asylums would, to my mind, do as much good as harm),—men who might well have been spared and saved to do good work in the world, but who now lie as helpless as the enchanter at the feet of Vivien in the hollow oak—

Lost to life and use, and name and fame.

II.

Since I finished the first chapter of this discourse of mine, some of the few friends to whom I confided my intention of committing my experiences to the dangerous form of the litera scripta have been inclined to remonstrate with me for my audacity. Indeed, they seemed to think that there was something very wrong about the whole thing; that I should in some subtle way be breaking a confidence which should be devoutly kept—with myself, I suppose; and that the secrets of the prison-house of lunacy should be as sacred as the mysteries of Ceres of old. Whether, when these papers shall have been published, they will punish me in the Horatian fashion, and forbid me to stretch my legs under the same mahogany, or tempt the fragile bark in their company, I cannot say. But I am at a loss to see my crime. I feel disposed to quote a saying of Shirley Brooks in Punch, which always struck me as one of his funniest, when, in answer to numerous inquiries why his famous paper was published on Wednesday, and dated a Saturday in advance, he simply wrote in his 'Punch's Table-talk,' 'What the deuce is it to anybody?' And I repeat what I said or implied in my first chapter, that as the strange experience recedes into the past, and the painful sense of insecurity dies out which at first it left behind, the blessed spirit of fun comes to my assistance, and the 'humour of it' affects me as much as Corporal Nym.

I rejoice in agreeing with a friend of mine, who, in talking the thing over, said to me, 'The worst of you is, you are rather brutally sane.' And the absurdity of any connection between myself and a lunatic asylum strikes me so forcibly that I begin to rub my eyes and ask myself whether it all really happened. It seems some degrees less real than it did even when I finished the last chapter. So I cannot get on the same standpoint as my friends, or discover that I am hurting my own feelings by my own disclosures, as they appear to think that I must. If I hurt those of anybody else it is neither fault nor affair of mine. There are unfortunately too many people in the world who cannot be supposed to have any to hurt. And to expect that a scribe should refrain from making capital of such an adventure is to ask too much of mercenary humanity. When various angry designs upon the law, for actions for false imprisonment, had given way to the reflection that the justice which got me into the mess was not likely to set me right afterwards, and it had struck me forcibly that it would be better to sit down and calmly to narrate my 'travels in the dark land' than to pay for the chance of redress, I grew very comfortable about the whole matter.

Men have travelled, and fought, and got besieged, and shut themselves up among the paupers, and done many strange things before this, for the mere purpose of writing books about their doings. But I feel sure that no man ever submitted to be treated as a lunatic with that view; for if he had he might never have escaped, had he been as sane as I, to tell his story. I know that for some time I might have been under the impression (which a friend of mine, who once paid a visit to the asylum, told me had been decidedly his) that the house-doctor, whose business it was to cure us, and above all to set us free, was one of the most remarkable madmen in the place. Well do I remember how, when I sank into a state of depression and absence of mind over the billiard-table on the tenth repetition of some especially dull old story of his, and quite forgot to score, this doctor reported me to my relatives, and I dare say to her Majesty's Commissioners, as having 'fallen into a dangerous condition of torpor.' Torpor was the word.

De Quincey himself, with all his power of eloquence and word-painting, might have found even the dreams of an opium-eater less difficult to fix and to describe than the marvellous fancies and dissolving views of hypochondria, when it passes from the domain of fancy into that of real illness. In that earlier and fanciful stage it may or may not be conquerable by that effort of the will which is so easy to preach and so hard to practise; but in the second it is, save by the action of what I suppose I must call—in days when a higher and a nobler Name is something out of date in the 'best circles'—the vis medicatrix 'Naturæ,' practically incurable. The doctors, who know what Galen knew and no more, but apparently believe in themselves none the less even for the teaching of Molière, are powerless before it. Their kindness of heart abounds—as, thank God, there is much of it everywhere—but their skill does not keep pace with it. One of the kindest of them whom I know, and I think the most sensible, told me that he had once under his care a lady who was suffering from hypochondria in a severe form. She recovered; and some time afterwards she met with an injury to the spine, of which she died in great pain. When she was dying she told him that her sufferings were as nothing to what she remembered of the mental pain of that first illness. And I believe it to the full; though we know that mercifully there is nothing we forget so soon as pain. Add to that indefinable and wearing agony the surroundings of a large lunatic asylum—beyond conception the most cruel place for such a malady—with medical supervision merely nominal, where all, with scarcely an exception, are regarded as incurably mad, and simply kept out of the way to save families trouble,—and the pen of a De Quincey would help me as little in the description as my own. I shall, therefore, begin quietly from the beginning.

In these coddlesome and unmanly days of ours it is
becoming almost rare to meet, in London life at all events,
with a man who is not more or less of a hypochondriac
about that unlucky scapegoat of modern times, his liver. It
is represented as such an ubiquitous, elastic, and sentient
being, that personally I am beginning to disbelieve in its
existence altogether, and regard it as a sort of 'Mrs. Harris'
in the human economy. Since the spread of what I may
respectfully call Andrew-Clarkism amongst us, the
humourist may find ceaseless matter for meditation at the
club dinner-table and at ladies' luncheon-parties in finding
out the exact number of glasses of wine (the quality never
seems to be taken into consideration, somehow) which each
respective liver will bear, and the relative size of the plate
of cold meat (or 'egg, its equivalent') which may be
consumed with slow mastication. The wine or the one glass
of cold water, which is undoubtedly better, must be sipped,
not swilled; and the general effect, though depressing, is
excellent if persevered in. That it is seldom persevered in
longer than Nature will allow, and that the patient after a
time rushes to the nearest and best-filled board under the
influence of uncontrollable thirst and hunger, and so brings
a grateful liver to willing reason, is probably the cause why
this modified Sangradism survives so long. The days of
alcohol are theoretically numbered, but I doubt if they ever
will be practically. In older and simpler times it was known
as wine to strengthen the heart of man; and why the
temperance doctors, who prove beyond dispute that alcohol
is not food, in forbidding it always instruct their victims to
resort to a corresponding increase of animal sustenance, is
beyond my academic logic. It implies a syllogism as much
outside of the domain of our old friend 'Barbara celarent'
as Macaulay's famous argument:

Most men wear coats,

Most men wear waistcoats,

Therefore some men wear both.

But the logic of medicine is not as the reason of other trades. I had been thinking of these things the other day when I went to church and heard the dear old story of Cana in Galilee. And no reverent mind will accuse mine of irreverence if I say that, in spite of myself, my thoughts shaped themselves into an epigram:—

A miracle of Love Divine

Changed all the water into wine:

Save me from miracles of men,

Who want to change it back again.

This is a digression, but very germane to the matter in hand. For a long course of inanition on the modern principle, not sufficiently combated by submission to Nature's clamorous invitations to eat, drink, and be merry, and on the other hand indefinitely accelerated by the fearful shock of a course of German waters, was the prelude to the illness into which I fell.

Never mind with what it began. It has been said over and over again that work hurts nobody, but that worry kills. Home troubles, perhaps, beginning with the death of a very near and dear relation under circumstances of exceptional pain, were in my case the real foundation of the mischief, which grows very fast by what it feeds on when worry supervenes. I had, unfortunately, no necessity to work, became less and less disposed to do anything, and more and more the victim of diet-tables and prescriptions, with all their sad concomitants of dyspepsia and want of sleep, and, as a common consequence, the abuse of that grim and baleful drug, hydrate of chloral. The well-disposed interior will revolt at the very memory of its hideous taste, and fly to warning and remonstrance. As day by day the illness crept upon me, and the weary phantom of Self—and Self from its most distorted and morbid point of view—absorbed at last every thought and every energy, the well-known 'differentia' of the illness, the ground was being comfortably cleared for the experience that was to follow. Bred in the careless modern school of indifference to higher hopes and feelings; never an unbeliever, I hope (remembering Dr. Johnson's saying: 'Sir, if he is an infidel, 'tis as a dog's an infidel; he never thought about it'), but practically living the life of one, I was without the one stay and rest which can carry men triumphantly over worse troubles than mine. I had to kill Self as all of us must who would fain rise upon the stepping-stones of the dead giant to better things, before my illness was to bring forth its fruit. I hope and pray that it has done so now.

It strikes me that I am preluding still. But I believe that my experience, thus far, will appeal directly to many hundreds of men; and I wish to warn them fully and fairly—it is my object in these papers to do so—under the present condition of our law, to what hypochondria may lead, if they carry it so far as to bore their nearest and dearest, justly desirous to be amused and comfortable in life.

Let me pass those fearful German waters briefly over. I arrived at Carlsbad one summer all alone and half worn out; and that salubrious spot wore out the other half with

generous rapidity. Every morning, in the small hours, when
I ought to have been putting on flesh in bed, I drank away
at some spring or another a fraction of my few remaining
pounds of it, in company with a long train of fellow-idiots.
The waters of Carlsbad work as neatly as Shylock would
have done; only they require a stone where the Jew was
content with a pound. Antonio was an arch-hypochondriac,
by the way; I wonder if Shakespeare, who is proved to have
been everywhere and done everything, had been to
Carlsbad and concealed an allegory? I saw at least three
doctors at the place; for my first fell ill, and my second
could never remember what spring he had ordered me,
being convinced that only one could hit 'my case,' and
changing it, therefore, every time.

O Karlsbader Wässer,

Wäret ihr nicht besser

Als eure Doctoren,

Wir wären verloren!

So ran an agonised distich I found written up on a rock
somewhere. But doctors and waters are much of a
muchness, I think. Yearly will Charles's Bath claim its
hecatomb; I know not why. Harrogate is as nasty, and as
dangerous. To my mind, of all the poisons distilled out of
the bowels of the sometimes harmful earth, these same
waters are the worst. Strength and weakness are convertible
terms for health and sickness; and that which weakens by
reducing maketh not strong. And at this point of my sermon
take warning again, ye hypochondriacs, and beware.

I returned from Carlsbad seriously ill, and I grew worse
very rapidly. The supposed reaction which is so
ingeniously claimed as the result of these nasty drinks—to
account for the natural fact that all but the herculean among
the drinkers grow steadily worse for some time afterwards,
and better again when the effects have passed off—failed to
show itself in me for some years. It did at last, no doubt;
and I may send a votive tablet to Carlsbad yet. I became, as
I said, a bore. I was passed on from doctor to doctor, and,
as one of them frankly said, each gave me another kick
down the ladder. On one of the steps only do I ask to linger
for a moment, and to thank the one among them, true friend
and good man, whose eye this may chance to meet, to
whom I owe as much as one man can owe to another in this
world. Only he and I, in this world, know what I mean.

At last I reached the lowest rung of the medical ladder
indeed; for what the wine-trade is to the man who has
failed generally, so I take it is the lunacy trade (with
marked and fine exceptions, of course) to the doctor who is
no good for any other 'specialty,' and knows he is not. His
province is the unknown; the law works for him; he is in
charge of a certain number of unfortunates, whom others—
not he—have pronounced 'mad;' he argues, when he
argues at all, backwards. He has not to say to his patients,
'Your words and thoughts are inconsecutive, your eye is
wandering, &c.; therefore you are mad;' but, 'You are mad;
therefore your words and thoughts are inconsecutive, and
your eye is wandering.' This argument has been absolutely
used in that shape with me; and I leave honesty to judge
what the effect was.

But I could not afford to be angry, for that would have been
'excitement' and madder still. The position in which you
put some of us—some of you—with the light heart of M.

Emile Ollivier—is a cruel and terrible one, indeed, for the man conscious of sanity, but under the ban, ladies and gentlemen. And believing, as I do, that I am one of the very few who can ever have come through such an ordeal as this with all his wits throughout about him, I cannot wonder for a moment that others have been content to sit down quietly under this most intolerable wrong, and to hold their tongues, lest 'excitement' should be again brought up against them. But I will not, that is all. With all my heart I believe in the grand old Sophoclean line, which used to console Mortimer Collins:

Οὐδεν ποθ᾽ ἑρπει ψευδος εἰς γηρας χρονον.

For the benefit for those who have no Greek: 'No lie ever crawls to old age.' And even in this coward world I believe truth is master when used as the one fearless weapon, for attack or for defence.

But I have been growing 'excited,' good my readers, and I beg pardon. Some of my friends are naturally afraid of any excitement on my part. It is not easy to avoid sometimes. After this storm that has swept over my life, there is a great strong current of righteous wrath that will run on deep down beneath it to the end, but not more deep than I mean that it shall be still. Out of the nettle danger I have plucked the rose of safety.

It was bitter winter when, as the beginning of the end, I was relegated to the care of a good-natured young village medico, with about as much knowledge of the buildings of the brain, I should think (and small blame to him), as of Cambodian architecture. He was a kindly fellow, and did all he could; but he dwelt in a tiny hamlet on the borders of one of the dreariest tracts of our forest-country, and I reflect with sorrow to what a stupendous extent I must have bored him. I am consoled by thinking that I must have been of great value to him in his studies, as he was trying his 'prentice hand in 'nervous' cases, to which he suspected himself of a call, on me; and I wonder he failed to catch the malady.

Goethe once said that the greatest of physical blessings is a big head with enough blood to feed it, and the greatest of physical trials the same head without the blood, whose place has to be supplied by all sorts of fancies, which of course take the most morbid form. In my case they turned, as they have in such thousands of cases, to religious hypochondria. There is nothing more difficult to explain away, on any Darwinian or Contist hypothesis of which I am aware, than 'phenomena' of this kind. They exist, and will have to be dealt with somewhere. The curious story of John Bunyan has been repeated constantly since his days. They were trying at the time. I was fully convinced that I was the wickedest man that ever lived, and even in my illness rather triumphed in the fact after the fashion of Topsy.

Looking back from my present vantage-ground, and conscious of never having wittingly harmed anyone, I cannot imagine why I arrived at so desperate a conclusion. I must have tried that poor young doctor sadly; for I never spoke of anything but my sins and my ailments, though naturally I am blessed with a keen interest in all sorts of things—quicquid agunt homines, almost. For my sins, to deal with which he felt to be outside his province, he sent to the clergyman of the village locality, who fled after five minutes' discourse; and, as I have learnt since, with a good sense for which I shall ever mentally thank him, wrote to some of my relatives to tell them to send me 'home' at once—dear, good, blessed old word that it is!—and save me from doctors as soon as might be. They preferred an 'asylum.'

As to my ailments, I had evolved from my inner consciousness, after a varied and polyglot experience of many physicians, from whom I had suffered many things, certain astounding theories about acids and alkalies, and organic and functional disorders, which were innocent of the slightest foundation in fact, but, as far as I can see, quite as well founded as those of the faculty. One of the Diafoiruses, I remember, who had been baroneted for his performances, entirely declined to pronounce on me at all anything but the simple sentence: 'O Lord, take him away—beef-steaks and cod-liver oil!' Had he said 'Burgundy' instead, I had reverenced him now fully instead of partially. For I was, in fact, starving, and that was all.

But let me not laugh too much; for what followed was no laughing matter. I was 'attended' at my forest-doctor's by a servant, picked up I know not where, who considered it his duty to cheer me by suggesting cribbage, with dirty cards, and watching me, in my room, night and day, till his constant presence drove me nearly wild. Three of the leading 'mad-doctors' of London, to whom I was carried in 'consultation,' had pronounced me to be abundantly sane, though exhausted and helplessly hypochondriac, and bound to recover. So said my young doctor too. And when, one evening, after a foolish exhibition of desolate misery (and it was misery), the moral responsibility whereof, if any attach to it, I am now quite content to lay at other doors than mine, a relative arrived, and, without any reference whatever to the skilled men of whom I have spoken, ordered my instant removal to 'another place,' the same young doctor-host told me that he would never have sanctioned such a step; but the relative had stayed but five minutes, left the order, and departed for foreign lands.

I was therefore 'removed,' half-dying, in a state of semi-consciousness, I can scarcely remember how, to the castellated mansion mentioned in my first chapter. The wrong should have been impossible, of course; but it is possible, and it is law. My liberty, and my very existence as an individual being, had been signed away behind my back. In my weakened perceptions I at first thought that the mansion was an hotel. Left alone in a big room on the first evening, I was puzzled by the entrance of a wild-looking man, who described figures in the air with his hand, to an accompaniment of gibber, ate a pudding with his fingers at the other end of a long table, and retired. My nerve was shaken to its weakest, remember; and I was alone with him! It was not an hotel. It was a lunatic asylum.

III.

Of what followed for the next few days I cannot say much; for my head was then so thoroughly weakened that I had almost lost all count of time. It was a very merciful weakness, for without it I do not think that a sensitive brain could have borne a succession of shocks such as I described at the end of my last chapter. There was a very large number of madmen in the place, which was avowedly regarded as an asylum chiefly for 'incurables,' whence I conclude that it was thought convenient in my case to take the extremest view of matters at once. So little was I myself able to realise that resort could have been had with me to such a step as this, that, strange as it may seem, some months passed before I knew that I was the inmate of an asylum. I thought, in the dazed state of trance in which I contrived to exist from hour to hour, that I was in some sort of establishment devoted to nervous patients, whence I should be removed in due course of time; though, in the vague and dreamy speculations which occupied my days, I was wont inwardly to wonder what possible effect for good those broken nerves of mine could derive from constant association with a variety of people who were 'nervous' to such a very marked degree. Their ailments used at times to cause me much inward perplexity. One of them used to rush wildly about the passages of the house—generally with a file of old numbers of the 'Times' under his arm, in all sorts of wonderful costumes, which he was very fond of changing, an Inverness cape and a velvet cap being his garments of choice—shouting out scraps of song in a discordant voice. Another always wished to shake hands with me, and recite medical prescriptions at hazard; at supper, when a number of us sate down at a long table to consume some incredible beef-sandwiches as a wholesome prelude to quiet sleep, he would finish by crossing himself and eating the parsley. Tobacco he was rather fond of eating, too, poor fellow. He is dead now, thank God for it; for even in his vagaries and in my illness he impressed upon me with singular force the idea that he was exceptionally a 'gentleman,' and a good one. A few days before his end—he died of Bright's disease, good reader; and he wanted something more, I think, than asylum treatment—I remember his expressing his dislike to sitting down at dinner in a lady's company without being properly dressed. One of the 'matrons' was in charge of us at the time; a kind-hearted, clear-headed woman, to whom I was to owe my first release (I was condemned twice to my fate). From her first I learned exactly where I was, and the sort of net that had immeshed me; and, after she had talked to me once or twice for five minutes, 'This,' she said, 'is a cruel and a shameful thing. You have no business to be here. Your friends should remove you instantly.'

But I am anticipating a little. I met this lady, happily for me, at a seaside 'house of ease,' to which some few of the patients were periodically sent from the 'Establishment,' as the asylum was euphemistically called (we were very refined and Pickwickian altogether, and our warders were our 'attendants'), for change of air. To obtain even that slight relief, an order from the magistrates, who execute justice and maintain truth—and in this case were connections or near neighbours of the head of the establishment—is considered necessary. No loophole for escape was left us which the law can sew up. For five fearful months I lived at head-quarters in the asylum, the whole morale of heart and mind being more played upon and shattered every day. I have described the ways of two of my companions. Another, with an abnormally large head of hair, had a way of skipping about the house with startling entreaties for 'baccy,' or singing to himself a favourite little song, which ran thus: 'Hey-diddle-diddle, I want some more beer.' Yet he could be consecutive sometimes, too, when one talked with him; and under the care of the same matron he sensibly improved, as, when I met him again afterwards—how shall in due course be told—he had sensibly deteriorated. He was mad, no doubt, quite mad, but very gentle; and I ask all good and reasonable people, on every good and reasonable principle, how such a malady as his can be bettered by constant association with other mental maladies of every sort and kind? For myself—I say it again—my physical weakness saved me, with the consequent incapacity of the brain to receive immediate impressions strongly. But the impressions were made, deep and enduring; and they come out afterwards in the light of health and freedom, as the photograph takes form and strength under the action of the chemicals. Now, happy and free, the horrors that were like dreams at the time seem to shake me as I write; and strongly balanced as I know my brain to be, I doubt if the companions who in sickness but vaguely frightened me, in health would not break me down. There is a very fearful responsibility somewhere for what was done to me.

Patients there were of other and of many kinds. There was one black gentleman from India who never spoke; but who used ever and anon to glare at me, and make one or two steps towards me as if meditating a rush. Then he would lick his lips with a very red tongue, sit down opposite me, calmly pull off his boot and stocking, and nurse his foot. I think that he had for me the greatest fascination of any of them; and I remember being at times under the impression that he was a wild animal in disguise. One poor creature there was whom I dimly but firmly believed to be an ape; truly, for my desire in writing these papers is neither to extenuate nor set down aught in malice. He was in truth, I have been assured, a gentleman of large private fortune; but never have I seen humanity so fearfully lowered. He was very ape-like, small and muscular. His chief employment was to sit over old volumes of the 'Illustrated London News,' which periodical was weekly sent to his address and taken in for him; to lick his fingers, and turn the pages rapidly over, crooning the while some horrible gibberish to himself in a voice quite inhuman, without two consecutive syllables or one ray of reason; to tear out little bits or whole pages of the volume, and throw them away with a triumphant yell, which curdled all my blood and improved the nature of my dreams, watched over as they were by two or three keepers, who would report me the next morning as having had 'a bad turn' if I awoke in the night, utterly nerve-shaken, under the influence of this living nightmare. This hapless youth was known by the name of 'Jemmy,' and was a standing jest with the warders, who delighted in playing in every possible way upon his ghastly idiotcies. For he was lower than a madman, far; he was a raving idiot. He would jump at times from his seat, mount on a chair, and play hideous symphonies upon the window-pane to the accompaniment of his own voice; once or twice, I am thankful to say, nature had its way, and he would strike a warder violently between the eyes. When he dealt out this measure, as once he did in my presence, to the servant whom I have described as with me in the forest, who conveyed me to the asylum, and there took service as a keeper—no doubt of personal affection to me—I was, I confess, inwardly but intensely gratified.

This was the worst of my companions, certainly; but there were others scarcely less uncanny. There was one poor old man, hopeless and harmless, who wandered constantly from room to room, or up and down the long dining-room, where it was the custom to herd some of us together, murmuring to himself odds-and-ends which I presume to have been original, snapping his fingers and making dreadful faces. His favourite burden was this—which, in spite of all I can do to drive it away, has taken a firm hold on my memory:

Gibbs is a beauty, and Gibbs is a louse;

Gibbs is a pig, and the pride of the house.

The second verse of the ditty running thus:

Gibbs is a beauty, and Gibbs is a bear;

Gibbs has no cap on the top of her hair.

This he would follow up by a delighted laugh over 'the Dowager Gibbs, the Dowager Gibbs!' and add, in a tone of pointed regret, 'A woman without a cap—it's indecent!' 'Miss Lloyd was a fine woman, a very fine woman,' was another of his favourite meditations as he tramped ceaselessly up and down. He had a younger friend in the house—he must himself have been well over sixty—to whom I contracted an intense aversion; a poor fellow who had a certain liberty about the place, and invested himself with imaginary dignities, acting as postman and bringing our newspapers to our rooms in the morning; superintending the work of the gardeners with an air of personal responsibility, and always reeking of very bad tobacco, and thrusting his confidences under one's nose accordingly. Among other duties he was allowed to score at our daily cricket-matches in the summer; and well do I remember how when I, weak of head and body, and with no business out of bed, but having yet some cunning at the game, joined in it at this evil place for the first time, I grew puzzled and angry at the astounding arithmetical results of my innings—I could scarcely stand, and the 'attendants' bowled a fast round hand at my legs—and failed altogether to appreciate the humour of the thing. I confess that, in the retrospect, I fail to appreciate the especial form of humour now. The postman and marker is dead too,—thank God for him again, and may the peace be with him that man denied him here! He and the poor old man I spoke of were, as I said, sworn friends; and their friendship showed itself in a series of hearty slaps and kicks cheerfully administered by the younger performer, the two apparently fancying themselves schoolboys, with the loud and sympathetic applause of the warders. The elder had been a University man and a scholar, and was still, at his better moments, full of odd scraps of talk and knowledge, and, in his Shakespeare especially, rather deeply read. And next friends and Commissioners and the law nursed his old age like this. There are more things on earth, ye people of England who live at home at ease, than are dreamed of in your philosophy. The less said, in this connection, of the other place mentioned in that famous quotation, I think the better. But nothing brings home the conviction of its reality so strongly to those who have suffered, as the absolute necessity for some other world; for some unerring court of appeal, before which the wrongs of 'the courts below' shall be signally and strangely righted.

The pudding-eater of my first evening, whom I introduced at the end of my first chapter, proved one of the pleasant features of the place. I find that I have written down the adjective seriously; let it stand. He was a great sturdy North countryman, without a vestige of sense or connection in his ideas, who was always occupied in imaginary architecture, discovering at the corners of passages or in the middle of a field, or anywhere, the most attractive sites for elaborate buildings, whose height and proportions he would proceed to indicate. He was always laughing in the heartiest and most infectious way; had a conscience and digestion apparently alike without fault, and might be set down by an observer as enjoying life without reserve under conditions which, I venture to think, would have soured Mark Tapley. Everybody liked him and was pleasant with him, as he was with everybody; and it is a matter for strange thought, what could have brought so hard a visitation on so simple a soul. Is it hard in such cases? Who can say? When I wrote in my first chapter that the mad seemed happy enough, I suppose I was thinking of this man; for the faces of most appear to me as I look back like a picture-gallery full of varied expressions of human sorrow, and sorrow debarred from expressing itself. I spoke once to a lawyer who was 'one of us,' who talked much to himself in an undertone, and would sometimes answer a question with a monosyllable, and asked him if he had been imprisoned long. 'Forty years,' he said, and turned away. Forty years! The answer came upon me with a shock no words can tell. I was feeling unusually well that day, or I should not have mustered courage to speak to him. I was working out my second sentence then, and knew where I was. And I did not believe in my heart, for I knew something of the law's ways by that time, that earthly power could free me. Nor did it, I think. I believed that I had forty years of life in me. Was I, too, to live them out there, and so? How much and how earnestly, if half unknowing, I prayed from my heart for death, with that unconscious cry of the creature to the Creator which flies up in spite of us in such straits as these, I do not know. I read the other day of a poor fellow in a public asylum (which I believe to be better than the 'private,' for the doctors have more the check of fear) who prayed aloud for death under the warder's hands. How many tortured souls have so prayed is written elsewhere, not here. From me the death that had been so near was then receding, and I seemed to grasp vainly after it to woo it back again. One day, led about the country roads weak and wretched, at a warder's heels, for the morning's constitutional, to look right and left of me for a deliverance that came not from the east or the west, to be idly and curiously scanned by the passers-by, but looking restfully upon every sane face that was not a keeper's,—I liked the mad faces better far than theirs,—I threw myself once upon my knees in the middle of the public road, with one silent heartfelt prayer—for what? For annihilation; for every form of possible existence seemed then to me a curse. Mad indeed, was it not? Nor need I say how mad I was then writ down. Yet it was within a few weeks of that time that my prayer was answered, in spite of myself almost, as I said before, and answered with life and freedom. Is there any one, I wonder, amongst our men in power who will be shaken by these words in the complacent selfishness of humanity, and be no longer content to pass those who have so fallen among thieves by on the other side?

The lawyer was not the patriarch of the place; for there were some aged men who had lived their lives there. One old gentleman, known as 'Daddy,' and a favourite butt with some of the younger warders—good-naturedly enough, perhaps; but I often felt that I should like to knock them down—was there, I believe, in the last century, and is not quite sure what George is on the throne. I was told that he never spoke at all for many years, until one day—he had never smoked in his life—he was by some means persuaded into a pipe. From that time tobacco became his solace and delight; for that he would ask anybody, and for that alone. His little 'screw' became an institution. The silent members of our corporation were very numerous;

whether they were silent always, or whether by degrees the habit crept upon them in that fearful mockery of companionship, will not be known here. I have said that for the first few days of my first imprisonment—to take up again the thread of my personal story—I was too ill and weak to observe or to care for anything. I think that I must have been in bed for a few days, dying alone; but that I do not remember. After that immediate danger had passed, I must have been one of the silent for some time; for I well remember the expression of astonishment which came over the faces of some of the warders in attendance when a letter was one day brought to me in the common room which had forced the passage somehow, and I answered to my name. The correspondence of the prisoners is conducted under difficulties. All letters, written or received, pass through the doctor's hands, whether opened or not I do not know; and those that they write go through him, not to those to whom they are addressed, but to the persons responsible for their imprisonment. There lies another royal road to the discovery of truth. A fellow-prisoner, who became a friend of mine in prison (it is the shortest and truest word to use), who was as sane as I, but, happily for him, stronger in health, conquered this difficulty by writing letters to every quarter whence he thought help might come, and posting them by various contrivances in the country villages when he took his walks and drives abroad. He won his freedom; and the first use he made of it was to bestir himself to win me mine. Does this read like 'England in the nineteenth century,' I wonder? Or need we go to the Alfred Hardys and Mrs. Archbolds of Charles Reade to tell us again that fiction is not so strange as truth? He imagined; I describe. Which is the stronger?

When I first broke silence on this communication from the outer world—it was from a club friend, I remember, giving me some account of old literary and dramatic mates, who seemed to have passed into another sphere for me—I was stupidly observing my surroundings from the depths of an old armchair. The 'Dowager Gibbs' was shuffling and chanting up and down the room; the patriarch was puffing at his screw; the man-monkey was howling and gesticulating, and tearing up the 'Illustrated;' the postman was grinding out indecencies, which haunt me, in a harsh strident voice; the good fellow, who is safe in harbour now, was muttering a series of prescriptions of potassium, bromides, and iodides, and other kindred horrors (he had been an eminent man in his time, I heard, and had suddenly broken down—how I hated the warders for their patronage of him!); the lawyer was making notes in a red pocket-book, or stealing from a plate surreptitious gingerbreads, of which he was very fond; and the whole Witches' Sabbath was in full play. The keepers told off to watch us were holding more consecutive, but not more edifying, conversation about horses and bets and races, which appear to absorb their faculties much as they do those of many higher minds, varying it with local gossip and bad language, and much rough horse-play at our crazy expense. I wonder sometimes what effect it might have had upon them, if it had dawned upon them that among their unconscious charges there was a 'chiel amang them takin' notes,' quite involuntary, but photographic in truth at least.

I should have had no place in that common room, I believe, except when I wished it; for I was on the footing of a 'first-class patient,' and had a private room of my own. Those who had not had no choice but to grow worse year by year from the enforced companionship that I have written down. But I was too ill to have wish or power of my own. I was absorbed for the time in the servant I have more than once mentioned, who was my master, and knew and rejoiced in it. He was soon tired of his duty, which was to keep me 'company' (Heaven save the mark!) in my room, and preferred to transfer me to the larger, where he might consort with his mates, and I with mine. The chief doctor, when I was at my worst, came to see me once a day. And I well remember the threats with which my 'attendant' would deter me, ill and broken as I was, from complaining of the life I had to lead. If he had known my illness and powerlessness to the full, he would have had no need to do it, for I did not know what I had to tell. But well do I remember how some words seemed to be struggling within me for utterance during the five minutes allotted me, to which I vaguely looked forward with a sort of daily hope of something; something which came not—justice, I fancy. I was tongue-tied by misery and illness, and my 'servant' stood behind the door while the doctor was with me. And so the days went by. Here I must ask my readers to remember that my brain was very weak, and that, as far as these warders are concerned, I am trying to disentangle the literal facts from my memory as exactly as I may. They are supposed to be the qualified nurses of the sick; they are men of the most ignorant class, without one single qualification for that duty—discharged soldiers, sailors, footmen. And they are the absolute masters of these asylums (of which I, remember, inhabited what has been called the best), and of the lives and liberties imprisoned there.

IV.

My first acquaintance with the warder whom I regarded—I
do not very well know why—as a sort of master-gaoler
among his fellows, was made upon my road to the asylum.
I was escorted to London from the forest by my adhesive
body-servant, and by the young doctor whose charge I was
leaving, who had formally certified my insanity. As I have
said, he told me when we parted that he held the step taken
to be wrong, and wished it to be avoided. I was ill, he
thought, and needed care. I fail to see, under these
circumstances, how he was justified in signing the
certificate. He was young, unskilled, a stranger to me but a
week or two before, and I had lived with his wife and
family. Whether any pressure was put upon him I do not
know, and had rather not enquire. It is enough for my
purpose quietly to state that I am to this hour in the dark as
to the details of the business, and that I was consigned to a
madhouse, against his will, on the order of a doctor who
did not believe me mad. Three authorities on lunacy had
stated but a short time before that I was in no danger of
being so. Nor was I—till the madhouse made the danger.
Such is the law.

He escorted me to London, and we parted there. At the
terminus the confidential warder met us from the asylum,
and took his place. The last I saw of him was that, as he ran
fast along the platform, he 'washed his hands with invisible
soap,' expressively, as of me and my concerns. He guessed
something of what he had done, I suppose, though I hope
not all; and thought that I was going forth into the outer
darkness for evermore. My companions were well fitted to
conduct me there. The forbidding personality of my special
servant is still at times a presence in my thoughts; and the

other afterwards was to haunt me still more. He was a rough, red-bearded, well-looking fellow enough—an old colonial squatter—and, as I remember him, very sufficiently good-natured and good-hearted. He was very fond of beer, and great at collecting shilling novels from all quarters. When in the latter days of my imprisonment he was told off to keep a special watch over me, I grew to shrink from and to dread him, in my very weakness, like a whipped child. He was kindly, but too big, and I was afraid of him. How many fears of the same sort must harass and perplex all those darkened lives is another of the sealed mysteries of the English Bastilles. I associated him so closely with my first coming; I remembered with a vision at once so dim and clear how he had curiously examined me from the opposite seat of the carriage as the train sped on in the darkening winter evening, through what country I knew not, to what destination I had no care to ask. When the doctor whom I had left had hinted where I was to go, I had failed to understand him. Had he told me in more direct words, I could not have believed in such a thing being done; I could not have believed in its possibility, as on looking back it baffles my understanding now. I have read many tales and many histories which turn upon the abuse of lettres de cachet in the famous ante-Revolutionary days. Will anybody tell me the difference? It seems to me that all that could be done by their means can be done 'under certificates' here and now, and legally justified afterwards over and over again. The Bastille itself could scarcely hold its prisoners more closely than the 'establishment' wherein I lived; and scarcely harder could it have been for any echo of complaint or suffering to reach the outer world. Buried and forgotten we lay there, like dead men out of mind. Of the farcical visits of inspection made by her Majesty's Commissioners I shall have something presently to say.

Their manner of discharging their solemn duty is, to my mind, in the whole round of wrong the worst feature of all.

Whilst I was being thus spirited away through the heart of London, with scores of warm-hearted friends within unconscious hail who would have raised a riot to save me if they had known anything of the truth, I knew as little of the fate before me as the inconvenient kinsman on his road to the old Bastille. Had I known, weak as I was, I should have resisted; and with what result? What is the result to those who do righteously resist? For there must be some who do. On my second apprehension, which I shall describe in its place, I should have known. But I was drugged by authority, as effectually and deliberately as ever was heroine of a novel, and brought back to my prison from the North of England under the influence of opium. More of this in time. Let me return to my first journey. There were my warders winking and blinking; my private domestic pouring into the ears of the other, who listened with the indifference of a man accustomed to the ways of nameless beings like me, his own version of my private history, and making grabs at me in the dark when we came to a tunnel, to create a prejudice in my favour. I remember dimly wondering what it was about, expecting the men to handcuff me, vaguely dreaming of the charms of bed and of a 'home,' speculating somewhat why I had none. Of that journey I remember little more, except eating savoury jelly at Waterloo Station—so oddly do trifles impress one in the most critical moments of life. The next turn of the kaleidoscope pictures me seated in an armchair, just before the episode of the pudding-eater, I suppose, interviewed by the ancient head of the asylum, who, having me there under certificate from my family, had no opinion to pronounce on my mental condition, but simply to accept me as a madman, worth a round sum a year to him, and be thankful. But for a

certain episode which I shall in due course relate, I might
not have found the man out. He was quite stupid, and had
so muddled his venerable brain with the contemplation—I
will not say the study—of insanity, that, after five minutes'
conversation, any two apothecaries from anywhere would
have 'certificated' him at once. He knew nothing on earth
about me; saw me for the first time under conditions not
perhaps exactly favourable to an impartial judgment; and
afterwards, as I have before told, paid me occasional flying
visits, which he spent chiefly in nodding and winking at me
in a knowing manner, and treating the few words which fell
from me as so many excellent jokes. He had heard that I
was theatrically given, and humoured my shattered
intelligence by taking every opportunity of telling me that
he had once taken his daughters to the Adelphi to see
'Martin Chuzzlewit' or 'Nicholas Nickleby'—I forget
which—followed invariably by a little anecdote of one
Grossmith, an old 'entertainer,' who was wont to imitate
Charles Mathews (whose loss we are regretting now) so
well that when Mathews once met him in the train and
heard him talk he said, 'If you are not Mathews, you must
be Grossmith.' I think that was the story; but I grew rather
addled over it at last, and am not quite sure. Grossmith the
younger, who has since that time made for himself some
name upon the stage, came twice from London to
'entertain' us. An old stage-lander, I seldom remember
feeling so severely critical. 'Hyperæsthesia,' I think, is the
medical alias for the quickening of the nervous perceptions
which so curiously accompanies, and yet contrasts with, the
odd sense of unreality with which bloodlessness of brain
invests everything. I listened to the performer's humours
like a man in a dream, with a bitter sense of unconscious
revolt as I recalled many happy evenings at the play, and
went drearily to bed, wondering more than usual how it
was all to end. By an odd flicker of the old flame, I

remember feeling as if it were incumbent upon me to go 'behind the scenes' and present myself, but could not make up my mind to it. What would the actor have thought had he come behind the scenes with me that night, I wonder! Some months afterwards I was watching him from a stage-box through the oddities of the 'Sorcerer,' and it brought back to me with a shock the fearful place where I had seen him last, and made me throw an involuntary look round me to see if any warder was on the watch. The feelings of fear and shame—for it has in one's own despite a sort of shame about it—that the experience left behind, died slow and hard. And a chance association like this would curiously awake them.

But I am keeping my old doctor waiting. He looked and moved, and I dare say tried to believe himself, the absolute incarnation of respectable Benevolence. The frock-coat, dark suit, and white cravat in the initial stage of strangulation, which are to so many people a sort of badge of a doctor's degree in divinity, law, or medicine, and the hall-mark of a good heart, carried out the illusion. He began to do good-natured things at intervals; I suppose from a spasmodic sense that he might as well try to cure a patient sometimes, instead of leaving them all entirely to the salutary effects of association. He once proposed to go through a course of Greek Testament readings with me, and we accomplished an entire chapter, but dropped the cure at that point. My power of reading Greek at sight appeared to impress him much, as by force of contrast with his insane patients it well might. But it failed to incite him to further efforts for my recovery and release. The Grossmith anecdote, to be taken at intervals, was an easier prescription. Though he had taken very kindly, however, to the work which he had accepted in life, he yet never gave me the impression of being altogether 'undisturbed by

conscientious qualms,' and of having been able to silence
the monitor which must have pleaded at times so loudly
within him. He was one of those men who never look one
straight in the face. And though he had constructed a little
chapel in the establishment, where services were held on
Sunday evenings, he did not attend those services himself.
Perhaps he may have feared that prayers for 'prisoners and
captives,' and the solemn appeals to Him 'who helpeth
them to right that suffer wrong,' might stick in his throat
like Macbeth's 'Amen.' He was happier in his own little
house, at some distance from the asylum, where he lived,
with none of the unfortunates under his immediate eye. He
pottered about among a large variety of baby greenhouses,
which he had constructed on patterns of his own, or made
geological investigations under his fields, where he had hit
upon a vein of quartz—or pintz, or something—of which
great things were to come. Little quarries were scattered all
over the place, and much lunacy must have been necessary
to support them. He was a great inventor, the doctor, and
was much distressed by the evident want of mental power
that I once showed by wandering helplessly from the point
when he was expounding to me a plan for some stove
which was to give heat without light, or light without heat,
or both or neither. I betrayed after a time an utter
unconsciousness of what he was saying, which I fear must
have outweighed in the balance my mastery of the Greek
Testament. Human nature is a parlous thing. In moments
even more confidential he explained to me how he had
been an inventor from his youth, and how one of the
greatest discoveries of Simpson of Edinburgh had in fact
been made by him, and by him confided to his ungrateful
colleague. I confess that, even in my sad condition of
mental darkness, I ranked this story with the class which at
school we briefly summarised as 'little anecdotes which
ain't true.'

This acquaintance with my doctor and his ways was of a late date, when kindly nature had given me enough of returning strength to be able to hold my own in ordinary talk, with only occasional relapses into the light-headedness which survived the first long delirium, when habit had begun to dull the edge of my helpless fear, and robbed the hourly associations of my life of something of their unspeakable horror. I was then hopeless of escape, and had grown, I think, indifferent to it, as to all who were supposed to care for me I had apparently become an object of indifference. In the morne désespoir which had utterly taken possession of me, I knew of no one to whom to appeal. Only those who had consigned me to the life could save me from it, and what was I to say to them? I was ill when they did it; I was ill still. Why should they be anxious to convict themselves of wrong, and of such wrong? And so in my misery I let the days go by without wearing myself out still more by idle effort, stupidly resigned

To drift on my path, like a wind-wafted leaf,

O'er the gulfs of the desolate sea.

The few visitors who fell to my lot had of course accepted their own foregone conclusions about my condition, and every external appearance of the place was comfortable to the view. Under the paternal care of such a dear good old man, with such pretty scenes to look at, and such nice gardens to walk about in, and an hotel-like sitting-room of my own, I was obviously wicked if I was not very happy. Other visitors to that place there were, who might have taken another view of things. Two friends of mine, who had known me well in old days, came whilst I was there to see, as it happened, other inmates of the asylum. Both knew that I was confined there, and both desired to see me. One especially, who had his suspicions in the matter, made, as I now know from himself, every effort to make his way to me. But it was not permitted in either case, and I was given out as 'too ill' to see anybody. In the malady from which I was supposed to be suffering, the sight of an old friend's face might well be thought one of the best of possible prescriptions. I was not too ill. It was a lie. In all the facts of this piece of autobiography, I know of none more damning. The reports of my condition, and the changes of it, were to depend upon the doctors who lived on us, and the ignorant warders who took their first cue from them, and the three relatives who had taken upon themselves the responsibility for my imprisonment.

My first impressions about the 'principal' were funny. As I have said, I did not realise where I was. I did not know that I was in an asylum; I did not understand what the curious people about me were; the only living soul I knew in the place was the servant of whom I have spoken, whose presence there was perhaps partially the reason for my failing to grasp the situation. I had of course no ground for supposing that he was out of his mind, or means for understanding why he should quarter himself in an asylum. He assured me, I think, that where I went he would go, out of personal devotion. But as he took the opportunity of enrolling himself among the asylum-warders, and treated me with a curious brutality, happily limited by inadequate physical means to carry out his views—I was myself so wasted that a child might have maltreated me, and only a brute would—I must have my doubts upon the matter. It was with a strange sense of relief that one morn I missed him from the accustomed haunts, and learned that he had departed for India in charge of the black gentleman, who was translated ad eundem elsewhere, I suppose, as some of us occasionally were. It is a comfort to reflect that the black gentleman was of a vigorous build, and capable of resenting impertinence. I hope that he availed himself of his opportunity, as the man-monkey did, and employed personal arguments. The fancies of my bewildered brain chased each other like shadows. Sometimes I thought that this odious being was Judas Iscariot (his surname remotely resembled the word 'Judas'); sometimes—when he had told me how fond he was of me, and I was trying to dwell upon the pleasant fact—that he was a brother of mine who had died in infancy, and come back to love me in the absence of anybody else. Chance likenesses were enough to invest any of the weird faces round me with a name and identity of my own making; and when at night thick-coming dreams of the most vivid kind—through all of which, I am told, my sleep seemed as placid as a child's—invested phantoms with such reality that I was unable to separate mentally the visions of the night from those of the day, the confusion of brain through which I lived may be imagined. I have attempted to describe how, in their shocking lack of human characteristics, some of my companions assumed for me the semblance of animals. About my own identity I felt puzzled, and was a good deal occupied in arguing out with myself who I might be, from various insufficient data. The state is of course very common in delirium, and was in my case very natural. A short time before, I had been the possessor of home, family, name, and friends; and at the time when I needed all these most, I suddenly found myself an unregarded cipher, a worn-out garment cast aside, as unowned as 'Jo' at his crossing, and robbed of man's right of freedom without the mockery of a trial, when imprisonment was a form of cruelty which needs a new name. So completely was I forgotten, that when at last I came to life again, it was to find a three years' arrear of unopened letters piled up in my old chambers, for which no one during my illness had even taken the trouble to inquire. They read to me then like messages from another world. Some favourite pictures and my writer's chair—the unambitious 'Law library' which I had once owned, and a set of handsome and valued Harrow prizes, had vanished altogether, and 'nobody' was to blame. It was the doing of a company, I suppose; but I had clearly no business to reappear upon the scene. I did not like it, though.

Knowing myself in keep and hold, and not knowing why, it was natural that I should invest the asylum with the attributes of a gaol. I have said that I expected to be handcuffed in the train; and when on the first evening a fierce-looking man rushed at me with a dark-blue ribbon, asked me what I meant by not wearing one, and declared, with a sense of personal offence, that I was 'not the least like my uncle,' I took him for the master-gaoler, and mentally christened him, 'Rocco,' in the odd dramatic vein which would run through my thoughts. This blue ribbon, worn in honour of the University boat-race, and the fact that one of my first memories is that I found a hot-cross bun placed by my bedside for breakfast, in sympathetic honour of One who died to teach us love and mercy, are the two things which enable me to fix with accuracy the date of my imprisonment as about the Easter-tide, now nearly four years ago. The terrible probation that followed seems to me now to have cut my life into two parts, as completely as I am conscious to myself of its having changed my whole character, and stamped and remoulded it in a new and other cast. Such furnace-fires as these must do so. They make the common trials of our race seem ludicrously small, and I find myself looking with a certain quaint wonder at people who talk to me of their hard experiences of life. With what a sense of gratitude I find myself unembittered—however justly and strongly resentful, where other feelings would be out of place—regarding my fellow-creatures from the pleasantest point of view, and the world generally in the light of the laughing philosopher, I cannot say. Trials are like pills. The taste depends upon how you take them.

I have been very frank with my readers about the strange fancies which took possession of my brain. No one of them who has known what it is to lie sick of a fever, or has ever seen others lying so, will be surprised to read of them. But in a lunatic asylum these common signs of a common illness are called 'delusions.' I was talking once, during my interval of freedom, over the position in which I was placed, with one of the three doctors who had vouched for my soundness of mind, who has justly won for himself a great name among those who have in worthy earnest studied the diseases of the brain, as far as it is given to man to study them. He spoke to me of private asylums with shrinking and with dread; and in my hypochondriac days had warned me as a friend of the dangers that might await me. 'Travel,' he said; 'do anything rather than give way. If once you find yourself in an asylum, Heaven help you!' And when I spoke to him later of the things that had been said of me, 'I know that word "delusions" too well,' said he, 'and the use that is made of it.' I did not, then. But when, after my final deliverance, I found myself accused by those who should have helped and shielded me in every way of being 'under delusions' as to their conduct towards me, I learned to know. I discovered this indirectly through others, and would not at first believe it. But it is true, like the rest of the story, and like the rest of the story is so set down. They say it everywhere, and they may be saying so still, and I have long known that they did not scruple to say it. There let that part of my subject end; for I sincerely trust that it lies outside of human experience. But it is a possible consequence, remember, of this abuse of law.

In the general state of confusion which, launched as I was into this very novel state of existence, took possession of my faculties, and seemed almost to supply a meaning and coherence to the old rhyme,

Supposing I was you,

And supposing you was me,

And supposing we all were somebody else,

I wonder who we'd be!

the raison d'être of the old physician puzzled me exceedingly. Sometimes I took him for a superior being in charge of the prison, sometimes for a divine, sometimes for the Evil One, and sometimes for a butler. When labouring under the last impression, I resented some question he thought it his duty to ask me, and his attempt to bar my peaceful passage from one room to another. I am afraid that I took him by the collar and put him against the wall— perhaps, under the circumstances, a pardonable excess. The assault was not dangerous. There was nobody living at that moment, I think, who could not have knocked me down with his little finger. But from that time I was regarded, and entered in the books, as 'homicidal.'

V.

A letter has reached my hands about these experiences of mine, written in a courteous spirit, but supplying so singular a comment on my story that I shall answer it here. It is from a specialist, who has obtained, I conclude, some eminence in the treatment of insanity; for it encloses for my study, in the form of a pamphlet, a presidential address on the subject delivered by him two or three years ago. With a few points in his letter I must deal, for they are as curious an instance of what schoolmen call the ignoratio elenchi as I am likely to meet. 'The writer in the 'World,' he says, 'confesses himself in various passages to have been insane.' He suggests that I may possibly be 'merely a clever romance-writer;' but, deprecating my 'able onslaught on those medical men who have the dire misfortune to be engaged in lunacy practice,' adds that if my story is genuine I am 'bound to offer some suggestion as to the proper mode of treatment of the unfortunate victims of brain-disease;' and that as I have entered on a 'destructive course, I am in duty bound to finish by a constructive attempt.' Now for my answer. In the heading of this narrative, and throughout it, I deny distinctly, deliberately, categorically, that I have ever been insane; and I say that the fancies of delirium or hypochondria are as clearly to be distinguished from those of madness as midday from midnight, on a very little close observation, by every honest and unselfish mind. To send them to an asylum for treatment is the best way to turn them to insanity. I have been perfectly frank about my 'delusions,' for I remember them all, as had I been mad I should not. A man may doubt if he is in his mind or no; he cannot doubt whether or not he has been. The writer of the letter takes advantage of my having been in an asylum, as some of the friends who placed me there have done, to argue that I was mad. It is the favourite fallacy of the cart before the horse. It proves me to have been 'legally insane,' of course, and I give the phrase for what it is worth, with a contempt no words can measure. The doctors who made themselves the instruments of this wrong were two young village practitioners who never made any study of the matter, and one of them never saw me but five minutes in his life, when I was too ill in body to mark his face. Is this a state of law that should last? Is this a thing that should be let alone? Read some of Ruskin's 'Fors Clavigera,' gentlemen, and get rid of some of the selfishness which is the dry-rot of mankind, for which a placid acceptance of the wrongs of others is only another name. Scourge the money-changers from the temples, in the warrior-spirit of Him whose name we still bear. The very pamphlet before me speaks of nothing so much as of the special knowledge required in dealing with insanity; yet any two apothecaries may make a man mad in law. Let the very possibility of it be abolished. There is the first part of the reform which the writer wants me to suggest, for which in my first chapter I warned him and all others that they have no right to ask me. I am neither Home Secretary, Commissioner, next friend, nor medical man; and it is no answer for the author of a book to say to his critic, 'Come up and write a better.' 'Ne sutor ultra crepidam,' quotes the writer in his pamphlet; and it is true of me as of him. It is only my clear duty to set down, in words that shall burn, if God will send them to me, the breathing thoughts that spring, too deep for tears, out of my terrible personal experience. For this is no romance, but a commonplace reality. I have said with whom the responsibility for the reform lies: with the Home Secretary and Commissioners, and with the leading men in law and medicine who allow these things to be. When Sydney Smith said that nothing could be done with a corporate body of men, because they have neither a 'soul to be damned nor a body to be kicked,' he may not have been as right in the first clause as in the last. Souls may one day prove as divisible as the electric light; and before the Court beyond, to which I, and others who have suffered like me, from our very heart of hearts appeal, it will be of no use to plead a limited liability.

I will go on with my suggestions of reform, though I am not bound to do so, for I believe the key to be simple. The lunacy laws are made in the supposed interests of relatives, not the sufferers themselves; and all is done to 'hush up,' not to expose. Why? There is nothing to be ashamed of in insanity; but in their utter selfishness friends shrink from the supposed consequences to themselves if the thing is 'talked about.' As if it could ever be anything else! The birds of the air will carry the matter; and all that these people gain by it is to have the increasing sect of the 'Head-shakers,' as a friend of mine has pleasantly christened them, tongue-wagging more and more behind their backs, and saying, 'Ah, poor people! madness in the family, you know.' And it serves them very justly right. I know these same Head-shakers well, and know well enough that they will never allow me to escape from the consequences of the past, such as they are. 'There was something in it, you know; he was very queer. Pas de fumée sans feu.' Proverbs are either the greatest lies or the greatest truths; and in 'society' certainly this is one of the first sort. I was caught in the act of laughing at a play of my own only the other day, and I hear that a head-shaker spoke of it at the Mutton-chops Club afterwards as a melancholy sign of my mental condition. They congregate much at some latter-day clubs, the members of this sect; and, in the absence of natural material in that way, they tell each other what to think, and then go home and think it. Applied to literary work, the result sometimes comes forth as 'criticism.'

Let no man, then, be imprisoned for insanity till his state has been fully and carefully observed for a certain time; nor then, unless the certificate has been signed by two, or more, well-qualified and practised men, one of whom at least should have known the patient well and long. Let private asylums, where it is in the interest of the proprietors to keep the patients as long as they can, be swept away. I have known the enrolment of new patients on their books—may the poor people be helped, and those who place them there forgiven!—cited with as much pride as that of new boys at a schoolmaster's. Let public asylums be substituted, where it is in all interests to have as few patients as possible, instead of as many, and to dismiss them as soon as may be. Let the harmless, of whom there is a large proportion, be kept out of asylums altogether. Who knows what cruel pain the associations of their life may hourly give them? Let publicity take the place of hushing up—which never did any good in the world whatever—to the fullest extent. Let the warders (whom I have postponed for the present in deference to their social betters) be carefully selected for character and kindness, and be what they should be— nurses of the sick. Let the Commissioners, if they are to go on existing, read their duty in a different way. Further, let severe criminal penalties attach to every abuse of the reformed Lunacy Law, and let every facility be given to the sufferer as against doctors, relations, Commissioners, anybody, be he great as he may. At present the law, with all its intricate machinery for good or ill, fights dead against us: with my correspondent's plea for the sensibilities of those engaged in this line of practice, I am not much concerned. They need not adopt it if they do not like, I suppose. They follow their profession for profit like the rest of us, and have no need to pose as philanthropists, or ask for sympathy. 'Il faut vivre' would be their best explanation of their work; and I know of no case in which the great Frenchman's answer would come with more crushing force, 'Monsieur, je n'en vois pas la nécessité.'

If these suggestions of mine, which I did not propose to offer, savour rather of the destructive, to use my correspondent's phrase, it is because destruction is the only reform possible; and to patch up the old system is like mending worn-out garments with older cloth. When reform, utter and complete, has been devised and carried out, insanity may be 'eliminated'—I quote the same writer again—more than he thinks; for a blessing may fall on men's efforts which seems very justly denied to them now. As long as this form of false imprisonment is possible, as long as scores of sane men and women are being maddened in private asylums, and hundreds of mad people being driven madder, insanity in England will not decrease. As for its proper medical treatment, I have nothing to do with it and nothing to say to it. I take up my correspondent's address at his desire, in the hope of learning something, and this sentence is among the first to catch my eye: 'Voisin says that in simple insanity he finds certain alterations in the gray matter of the cerebrum, consisting of minute apoplexies, effusions of hæmatin and hæmatosin into the lymphatic sheaths, infarctions, atheroma, capillary dilatations, and necrosis of vessels, and certain changes of cerebral cells.' Quite so. It may be all very true; but I can offer no suggestions as to medical treatment based upon these remarkable assumptions. When, shortly before my final removal, I was allowed to see a relation of mine at a town at some distance off, the principal objected to the permission being too often given, because conversation carried off too much white matter from the brain. I distinctly assert that he said 'white,' because, by connotation of the statement with Voisin's valuable remarks, it will appear that the 'gray' remained in my case unaffected. That neither hæmatin nor hæmatosin has been effused into my sheaths, that my capillaries remain undilated, and that I am proudly conscious of having escaped both atheroma and infarctions, I must ask my readers to accept my word. What abominable nonsense is all this! And how soon may such nonsense degenerate into evil. In another part of the same pamphlet I find the writer presently citing this Voisin's recommendation of the 'strait waistcoat' on the ground that the patients like it! There, I think, it is as well to lay the treatise down.

To take up again the thread of my personal story, I have described how I was called 'homicidal.' Where my 'voices' came from, to which I alluded in my first chapter, I never understood; for indeed I have not the faintest notion what they mean. They are used as a yoke-horse with 'delusions;' and being simply nonsensical, they admit of no possible answer. As far as I can remember, after old Diafoirus had asked me a variety of questions to find out the especial form of madness for which my friends had committed me to his tender mercies, and became naturally more puzzled as he went on, he suggested 'voices' as a last desperate resource; and I, being rather tired of the business, and having thus far been unable to admit a single 'symptom' propounded, jumped at the solution as being purely idiotic. I presume that I must have admitted that at times, when I am alone and doing nothing, I am able to fancy to myself the speech and address of absent friends. Heaven knows I needed the fancy there. It struck me as a harmless admission; and when I was once afterwards gravely informed that 'voices' are about the most dangerous and incurable sign of mental alienation, even in my extremity I could not help being tickled by the profound absurdity of the whole thing. 'Voices,' said my friend of the Inverness to me one day in a moment of confidence,—he too was able to discourse pleasantly enough of old college-times, poetry, and other matters when he chose,—'they are always bothering me about "voices," and I don't know what the devil they mean.' This man has been a hopeless prisoner for some time; but he was so far wiser than I that he only admitted to hearing voices indoors; I rashly allowed that I heard them quite as often out of doors as in. I hear them often when I am hungry, summoning me with much emphasis to my meals.

This idea of 'voices' was in my case a suggestion of the doctor's, thrown out innocently enough, perhaps, in the first instance; but it did me in my illness fearful harm. It may be felt by all who know how much, at the best of times, some old tune or scrap of odd verse will haunt and worry us, with what tenacity this fancy, once implanted, would take root and bud in a brain always active and imaginative, and then wearied and overworn by long weakness, and incapable of the brave effort by which alone such contemptible nonsense could be shaken off, amid its grotesque and terrible surroundings. Harried and bothered about fits, voices, delusions, white matters and gray; ill beyond belief, and longing for nothing but good food and rest, but 'watched' night and day; speculating what and who all these people might be; irritated by the doctors and insulted by the attendants—vigorously kicked by one of them one morning, I remember, when my hands were too weak to do their office, and I did not dress myself quick enough to please him—that I should be here now, sound and strong, I may well attribute to some Power above the selfishness of men, which will not suffer these infamies to go too far. After the usual fashion in such cases, the doctor of that place may now claim credit for my 'cure.' I will show, before I have done, how he cut himself off, by his own deliberate statement, from the possibility of claiming it. Over these 'voices' of his I brooded and brooded till they assumed some thing very like reality. I thought in my wretchedness of some dead and gone who would have shielded me from this with their lives, till their unforgotten 'voices' became at last a very part and parcel of my individual being, if a certified madman may presume to claim it. They comforted and yet they haunted me, till at last I can almost believe that they became to me guardian angels, like the 'voices' of Joan of Arc. Small chance would she have stood in the hands of British specialists. England might have punished her worse than by fagots if she had handed her over to them. For me, had I to choose again between the most painful death and another term of imprisonment in the asylum best beloved of the Commissioners, I should scarcely hesitate a moment in my selection of the first. These 'voices' of the doctor's creation were to be cast in my teeth again and again. One of the three questions vouchsafed me by a Commissioner, during the whole period, related to them; and when I say again what I said in my first chapter, that they are the worst piece of humbug of all, I believe that I speak the truth, which is difficult where all is humbug. I have his leave to quote here the words of a friend's letter written about this history of mine. He spent one night at this same asylum, upon a visit there to a 'patient': 'Well may you say there is but one thing that can enable a man to bear such a trial. I often wonder how I got through that night, and how it was I did not find myself between two keepers next morning. I am sure I heard voices enough, but they were holy ones.'

This friend, who was not allowed to see me, was on a visit to a brother of his, whom I have described as having interested himself in my release. He had first been spirited away to another asylum (from which he was afterwards transferred), when his brother was but a few yards distant, knowing nothing of what was being done. He knew his brother to be sane, maintained it throughout, and at last succeeded in releasing him. A few facts in the story are a good pendant to mine. The victim in this instance had been engaged in all the worries of an election, when some friend took him to consult an eminent mad-doctor, who owned a private asylum in London. The doctor said that he thought him out of his mind. My friend went and demanded his reasons. The answer was that throughout a long conversation he had shown himself perfectly reasonable and consecutive, but on going away he had taken up the doctor's hat instead of his own. Forcible as this argument was, it was not enough, even in the opinion of relatives, to shut the man up for. But on a later occasion he became excited about something, and the same authority was again privately consulted. No information was given to my friend; but early in the morning this doctor sent two keepers from his own asylum, ready to wait for the result of an interview between the patient and two doctors, suddenly sprung upon him (one an utter stranger), under whose certificates he was then and there removed. When my friend heard of it, he took steps at once, but found that he could do nothing. The law provides that the two certifying doctors shall not be partners. One of these was in the habit of taking the business of the other in his absence. 'This was his partner,' said my friend, when looking about for redress. 'Not a registered partner, I am afraid,' was the legal answer. The Common Law Procedure Act, I fear, has failed to abolish special pleading, or to efface from the lesser legal mind the delusion—may I use the word?—that the object of Law is to defeat justice. [1] For some time the prisoner remained in this asylum; and he so far justifies the

Commissioners in their preference, that he describes that where I was confined, to which he was transferred, as good in comparison. In that other place he had no room of his own, and was herded, always, with all the mad indiscriminately. The only exercise they were allowed was within the walls of the grounds, the asylum being in London. He was denied pen and ink; but he saw the warders do such things that he contrived to pencil down some notes of what he saw, and succeeded at last in obtaining the materials, and writing to the Commissioners of what he had seen. 'We' were allowed to write to the Commissioners, if we found out our right. How many such letters we contrive to write, how many are sent if written, how many read if sent, how many acted upon if read, I do not know. In this instance these ordeals were all passed; for the Commissioners came, made an enquiry, and did—nothing. But the objectionable patient was removed to another place, where I met him during my second term. Sane patients must be in some respects a trial. I understand that my old doctor frankly complains that I was the greatest bore whom he ever had in his care, and I believe it; though at the close of our relations he did not seem too anxious to get rid of me. We saw very little of each other then, my fellow-prisoner and I, for it might have been awkward, but enough to recognise each other's sanity. His brother was working hard for him, and at last two impartial doctors were sent down from town to enquire into his case. 'We' have a right to demand that also, I have understood since; though how but by a miracle we can use that right, I do not know. When it is gained, of what service is it likely to be in such a place, prejudiced as the new doctors must naturally be,—over-anxious as the victim must be, who dares not be excited, and therefore natural,—painful as the cross-examination is? Nevertheless, in this case the two doctors, one of them famous in 'nervous' cases, certified this man to be sane, and left the certificate on record. It was kept back one month. I state the facts of this story upon my friend's authority, and by his permission.

My friend worked hard without, as his brother did within; and the hard-earned freedom was won at last, it matters not to tell how. When I was myself freed, I travelled for some time with my old fellow-prisoner, and never saw in him one sign or trace of insanity. An eminent medical baronet, with a curiously suggestive name, who is rather a patron of the establishment, and occasionally 'diagnoses' a lunatic at an odd hour, had, a little time before, solemnly pronounced from the tremor of his tongue—a member which, from my own experience, is apt to tremesce when one is nervous—that he was bound to have something dreadful—it matters not what—within a month. However, it is now very many months, and he has not had it. Slang is expressive sometimes. 'Bosh!' The baronet is said to be infallible at 'diagnosing' from the tongue this especial malady, which failed to appear. My friend had no illness. But those people had shaken his nerves, as for a long space they shook mine. The wickedness was done. How many are there who, in the face of such truths as these, can dare to disbelieve in Him who says still as He said of old, 'Shall not my soul be avenged on such a generation as this?' It is all very well to go to church and 'say' prayers, to quarrel about the form of your faith, the colour of your clothes, the number of your bows. Religion is an active, not a passive, word; and, like revolutions, is not made with rose-water. Do something, somebody!

Let me close this chapter with my first escape, as my readers may be well tiring of my story. After some months of stupid unconsciousness, I was sent for change to the seaside annexe of which I spoke. What the matron said,

after the short time of quiet observation which was all I
needed, has been told. What I felt when I learned from her
where I was, I need not say. Very good for me was the
association with her, who would rescue me from my
companions and my warders, to take me out with her for a
drive or a walk, in spite of the 'homicidal' tendencies of
which she had been warned. By her a relation was
summoned to see me apart from the associations of the
asylum, who had never seen me at all since the wrong was
done; and seeing, had no choice but to remove me, though
every obstacle was thrown in the way, by the
Commissioners even, who, shirking their own
responsibility, accepted for a salary, are glad enough to
throw it upon anybody. Very good for me also was the
association with the young doctor, a son of the principal,
and his wife, who lived in the next house in charge of the
'branch.' They had me in to sup or play whist with them in
the evenings, and said as the matron said. The young doctor
took it upon himself, in spite of orders, to let me sleep in
my room unwatched and alone, for the first time for many
months; and the relief was beyond words. 'I wish,' he said,
in answer to one of my questions, 'that you would simply
stuff all the food and drink you can get.' When I was again,
after some months of liberty, remitted to the asylum, I
heard that he had given up all connection with it, with the
regret with which one misses a personal friend. But I think
that I was glad to hear it, even then. He had a comfortable
berth enough had he cared to keep it; but he preferred to
buy himself a general practice and to go. I do not wonder.
Shakespeare was not as right as usual, when he said that
'conscience doth make cowards of us all;' for there are
some of whom it makes brave men. It is the worst of
enemies; but it is the best of friends and the most easily
conciliated, if we try in the right way. But I will moralise
no more.

VI.

The Head-shakers have a formal vocabulary of their own, which, after a certain experience, one begins to know by heart. It is constructed on the simple principle of giving a bad name to everything. This story has been called 'sensational,' when it is simply true. When a direct description of things as they are is sensational, things as they are are not things as they should be. I am told, too, that the story shows much disregard for people's feelings. It certainly does for mine, which are sensitive enough, and have been outraged beyond belief. When men condescend to think a little less of their own feelings, and a little more of theirs whom they shut up alive, we shall be on the road to amendment. Meanwhile, if anything I have written has at all hurt the natural sensitiveness of any who has suffered as I have, I am very sorry for it. To other feelings in the matter I am less than indifferent. 'Let the galled jade wince, our withers are unwrung.'

These chapters are not intended to be read as what my friend of the pamphlet calls them—an onslaught on the medical men engaged in lunacy practice. They are an onslaught on a crying national sin, and all who favour it. Among the men in lunacy practice are men who abhor the system on which any man may be writ down mad. Among them I have myself found one of the best friends I have had. He was one of old standing. He saw me when I was nearly at my worst; but he did not shut me up. He took me to his own house, and poured in oil and wine, like the good Samaritan he is. After a few days' entertainment with his own family, and at his own table—and he would never have of me one penny for his infinite pains—he assured me, and my friends too, that I was only a hypochondriac bound to get well. He would have made me so, if I would have consented to stay with him, in spite of a certain faith in hydrate of chloral, which I wish he would abandon. 'Hell in crystals,' my defining friend has called it. (Perhaps I may add here that the relation who should know me best testified to my sanity with as little variation.) I well remember how this warm-hearted doctor carried me off under his own protest to see an eminent dietist whom I would consult, so completely had the occult qualities of eggs and cold mutton been worried into me, and almost shouted as he left the room, in answer to the stereotyped, 'I hope you are very particular about his diet,' 'Diet be strong-worded; why, the man is dying of inanition!' So I was. But I was restlessly bent on my own ruin, it would seem; and 'Tu l'as voulu, Georges Dandin!' was the burden of my earliest asylum-dreams. The rolling stone would only stop in the breakers at the bottom of the cliff; and I found no Sisyphus to roll it up again till I played both stone and Sisyphus myself. Why, however, I was thus hastily shut up without any reference to so skilled a friend, and without my seeing him, I do not know. It was of him that I was thinking when I suggested what I believe to be one of the most important and easiest of necessary reforms—that no man should be 'certificated' without the assent of at least one valuable authority who knows him well, after careful personal examination.

I have gone back again in my story, and a breath of sea-air will do it good. Imagine me with the matron again. The change from the asylum and its associations to the little house by the seaside was very good in its effects. It was so for others than me; for the madmen there, poor fellows, seemed to me gentler and better in every way than they were when I saw them in the larger place. The warders were there to watch them, but had to be quiet and suppressed in a private house, and simply lived down-stairs as servants live. The breakfasts and dinners at the neat table, pleasantly presided over by a womanly hostess, were a relief indeed after my previous experience. That they should have proved so, when only she and I held consecutive conversation, and the other guests either kept silence or distracted us by strange words and antics enough to unnerve anybody, shows partially, I think, what the life which they 'relieved' must have been. The poor singer of the 'Hey-diddle-diddle' beer-song was in the house, and his way of carving his bread with his knife and fork 'intrigued' me much till the matron told me where I was. There, too, was the good parsley-eater, who died of Bright's disease; and it was there, just after I left the house, that he died. Only two or three days before he had to sit down to dine with us; and I remember the kindness with which the matron made him lie down upon the sofa, seeing the suffering of which he knew not how to speak, and sent him to his bed. A short time before he had calmly looked me in the face across the table, and pledged me in the vinegar-cruet, which he emptied. His brother, a clergyman, dined with us on a visit, and looked at me, I thought, with some curiosity. What was I doing dans cette galère struck more than one. Seen among the associations and scenes of the asylum, I believe that any one might perhaps have thought me unfit to be removed, so completely ignorant was I, in common phrase, whether I was on my head or my heels. Twice a day, in the regular course of things, were the seven or eight lunatics who composed the seaside colony marched out for a constitutional walk, with a pack of warders at their heels, in the direction opposite to the town and streets. Those walks were trying enough; at the asylum, among the country roads and lanes, they had been fearful. The matron saved me from them as much as possible, as I have said, with the most thoughtful and considerate kindness. She took me with her to hear the band upon the pier, and to stroll about with her, a prisoner on parole, among the holiday-makers of the popular watering-place; and those diversions, which seem dull enough in ordinary life, appeared to me quite exceptionally delightful. It was better when we talked of books and things and people; and what she said and wrote of me I have already told. In the evening she would rescue me from the rest to let me sup quietly with herself, when I did not go next door to supper or whist with the young doctor and his pleasant wife, who were in command of a detachment of female patients there. They, too, gave their opinion; and in the face of many remonstrances from quarters where I might least have expected them—in the face of the principal's opinion that I was a very dangerous person; in the face of her Majesty's admirable Commissioners, not one of whom I had to my knowledge so far seen, but who were well armed with the 'notes' of the warders—I was taken for the time away, and made a free man again. O spirit of Mr. Justice Stareleigh! 'Nathaniel, sir? How could I have got Daniel on my notes, unless you told me so, sir?' If the soldiers, sailors, tinkers, tailors, of the establishment had it down in their notes that I was mad, having been told so, to begin with, by their employers (who dilate on the delicacy of brain cases, yet trust the reports of ignorant men), how the deuce could I be anything else? Yet there was more than one of them, for all that, who did not believe it, and had the courage to say so. I will give no clue to their identities; for they might be dismissed retrospectively, if they are still in harness, for such a breach of duty. It would be the best thing that could happen to them, perhaps. The hardest part of the whole snare to me was, that I, who would not hurt a dog if I could help it, was represented as 'violent' when I was weaker than any dog. It was enough to deter any but the bravest

and kindliest from trying to help me; and I have no choice
but to suppose that that was the object.

But the 'violence,' and the rest of it, was too palpable a lie.
The deliverance came. Over the months which followed
before I came to be imprisoned again, matron and young
doctor gone—good plants flourish ill in such a soil as
that—I wish to pass as lightly as possible. They would have
chiefly to do with home matters which have no place in
such a story as this, and only concern consciences to which
I would have nothing to say. I have done with them—let
them alone. The period of my freedom lasted ten months. I
spent the time in aimless wandering from place to place—
among the bathers of Trouville and the playgoers of Paris,
in the hotels and streets of London—in a fashion which
would make a story by itself, were this the place to set it
down. The shock with which I had learned what had been
done to me had shaken to the centre what nerve the
'treatment' had left me. Night after night I did nothing but
dream, dream, dream of the asylum and its terrors. The
warders, whose faces I knew so well, were always behind
me; the antics of the madmen were re-acted with merciless
fidelity. The sense of utter helplessness in the hands of
mad-doctors, which the experience had left upon my mind,
would leave me neither night nor day. A traveller's chance
allusion in my hearing to 'Bedlam let loose,' or a
whimsical song about 'Charenton' in a French vaudeville,
would drive me out of the station or the theatre in helpless
fear of I knew not what. If a gendarme accosted me at night
in the streets, I shook all over in the expectation of being
removed to a French asylum. If I saw an advertisement
relating to an asylum in a casual newspaper, it was to lay it
down in terror. There seemed to me but one power in the
world—the power of the lunacy 'law.' Such is the
confidence which our vaunted system, which professes to

know no wrong without a remedy, could inspire in one who needed its protection so sorely as I. In one respect its might was certainly vindicated, for, abroad and at home, I thought that it could reach me anywhere. I kept these fears of mine as much as I could to myself; for to talk of them might be, under the circumstances of my life, to be shut up at once again. But it was a fearful trial. I was utterly cowed and frightened, and I was afraid to face anyone; for I thought I read in every face a knowledge of my story. Except by an occasional desperate effort, I could force myself to meet no one. But ill as I was then, and full of fancies, not one of the old friends who saw me imagined in me a trace of insanity. That I know. In Paris especially I found one old literary friend, to whose rooms—from that odd thing called sympathy, I suppose—I was able to go more often than anywhere else, though seldom enough, Heaven knows! I have often wondered since what are his real thoughts in the matter. In theatres and hotels, in streets and in cafés, seldom allowing myself to sleep more than one or two consecutive nights in the same place, from the fear of being 'taken,' and, when I did stay, afraid of going to my room and then of leaving it—I dreed this dreary weird chiefly alone. And by the odd irony of the whole thing, this was the time when I was indeed nearest to madness, and really required careful watching; not that of warders or of repression, be it understood, but of the affection which is unhappily not made to order. I had been called suicidal and homicidal when I was no danger to anybody. Now thoughts of suicide did indeed take shape and form in my mind. In that there was no madness, for the impulse which madness supplies to carry these wretched thoughts into effect failed me always, and so saved my life. Yet there was not a day at last when I did not leave the house with the intention—if I could only find the needed courage—of bringing this impossible existence to an end. I knew that I was not going to die; but I believed that, after the line of treatment so shamefully adopted once, to save trouble, there was little chance of escaping a second condemnation if I did not die. And the event proved me miserably right. Have I not cause to say that I have no special call to spare the susceptibilities of others? I have no respect left for Pickwickian feelings— none.

London was but a repetition of the story of Paris. I struggled to the theatre once or twice. One night I hid myself at the back of the pit to listen to a play of my own which had just been brought out with some success— written, of course, some time before. I thought publicity dangerous, and wondered stupidly if I had ever written such things myself. After some months in the country, where I tried to make a home-life in vain, and wore myself out more and more in long solitary walks, haunted by every kind of nervous fear, I went back again to London in despair, wondering if, as I had no courage to die, this would not in some way end itself by sheer force of exhaustion. It would not, for I was very full of life still. I let nobody know where I was, for I had no strength or care to write, and no one with whom I cared to communicate. Besides, I was afraid; and wandered from one hotel to another with a sort of hope of having become nobody. I had forfeited my individuality in the asylum; why want it back again? But I had to be accounted for, and one day at the Crystal Palace I found myself watched again by a 'gloomy man'—not with a yataghan, but a newspaper. Of course I thought he was a keeper, as I had been expecting that for some time; but he was only a detective. He was not very unlike some whom I have seen in plays, for he allowed me to detect his mission in a moment; and it gave me a certain grim amusement to lead him all over the gardens on a very unpleasant day, taking the most obvious notes of me that I ever saw, in an obtrusive red pocket-book. I strolled to the verge of the salt flood at the bottom of the gardens (not deep), where the antediluvians dwell, lingered about, and looked as if I meant to jump in. He showed no intention of interfering, but watched with interest from the opposite shore, and nearly filled his pocket-book. Then I disappointed him, turned away from the precipice like Box the printer, went to the refreshment-room and ate an ice. This bothered him a good deal, but he noted it down. In the train he got into a carriage conspicuously remote from mine; met a mate in London to whom he communicated his ideas; and, after watching me partake of a melancholy dinner in Lucas's comfortable coffee-room, while he dallied with buns and beer in the front shop, the two followed me to Mr. Hare's pleasant little theatre—I had never dared, after the lowering effect of the associations of the 'establishment,' which seemed to sink me in my own esteem, to raise my eyes above the pit—sat behind me, and watched my conduct in respect of Gilbert's 'Broken Hearts' with a regretful desire evident in their own minds for 'something spicy;' then saw me safe to my hotel for the nonce, and departed with a conscientious feeling of having done their duty detectively, and having entirely escaped my observation. Were they primary scholars in the work, I wonder? And which kept the more accurate notes, the watcher in his book or the watched in his head? Nothing surprises me more, as I think over all that dreary time, than the singular acuteness of observation in me, which no date or detail seems to have escaped. 'Hyperæsthesia,' I suppose, or derangement of the white matter. Perhaps it was an infarction.

Well, by the superhuman exertions of Inspector Bucket I had been tracked to my lair, and a doctor descended upon me the next morning, and asked me a few more questions.

But he was the one of whom I have spoken as having given a worthy brain to earnest work, and having so signally condemned asylums and delusions. No man could have been more kind and wise. He might well have been deceived into thinking me mad, I think; for by this time, with voices, delusions, visions, and all the nonsense drummed into me, I had well-nigh begun to think myself so. I had hardly any clothes with me, as I wandered with the impression that there must be a full-stop somewhere near. I had not brushed my hair; I looked utterly dazed, and had taken refuge in the smallest room on the topmost story of one of our largest hostelries. If I had been charged as an escaped convict, answer had been difficult. He was not deceived, though, and ordered the rest of mind and body which is sometimes as vain a prescription as port wine and sea-air to the wasted pauper. Failing better roads to it, I was sent off to a hydropathic establishment in the north, once more in the charge of a body-servant, who was not to lose sight of me upon the road. Ay de mi! all the hopeless old story was coming on again.

I knew that palace of the water-cure well. I had known pleasant days there in happier times, when I thought I would go thither and bathe for no special reason, and had amused myself much with the whims and oddities of the place; all the people 'going to Gravesend by water,' as Sir George Rose used to say. It had been the property of a kindly Scotchman since gone, who has left me pleasant memories of his home-circle and his private stock of 'whusky,' which he administered to me freely at night, when the water-washers were gone to bed, after instructing me in the theoretic virtues of abstinence in his council-chamber in the morning. Now, like other places of the kind, it had lost its home-shape, and passed into the impersonal hands of a company. The presiding medical authority was

now a different man. I wonder if he dreams of me
sometimes? The first night after my reaching the place a
crash came. I could bear this espial no longer; and the
dreams of dead dear ones had become so vividly mixed
with the nightmare horrors inherited from (what shall I call
the asylum?) Pecksniff Hall, that I never knew half I was
doing. The professional name for dreams, as I said before,
is 'visions.' Dreaming that a warder was upon me, and that
a ghost was telling me to run, I jumped up in my sleep and
rolled over the nearest banisters. The fall was not severe,
and the 'desperate attempt' failed; for I only broke a rib and
stove in my breastbone, which proved afterwards handy for
the warders to work upon. I was put to bed for a time and
taken some care of; and before long was able to drive and
stroll about again, and join in lawn-tennis. But the dream-
fears and the daily terrors haunted me still; and I still
shrank from everybody. At last came the realisation of my
constant fear; and I fell into a fit of light-headed
wandering, and began calling out at intervals various silly
things. What should have been done was to nurse me and
pour wine down my throat, and apply the common means
of homely restoration. What was done was this: the stout
bathmen and servants of the place were sent to hold me
down; and I was gagged, and left gagged, till the blood ran
down from my mouth. Then came two strange doctors as
before, of whose names and faces I am ignorant, and were
instructed by my 'friends,' I suppose, to sign a certificate. I
was then given a strong dose of opium, and a summons was
sent to the Master of Pecksniff Hall, who despatched two
stout warders northward by the train, for the impounding of
my Herculean frame. One was the good-natured colonial;
the other a man whom I held in especial aversion, a fat ex-
footman, who afterwards reported his work as 'very good
fun,' and had a particular aptitude, when I was lying
helpless in bed, for jumping on my breastbone and half

throttling me. A fancied resemblance in his moony
countenance to an historical face made me, when I was one
day dreamily contemplating him from bed, connect him
vaguely with the Orton family; and among the dramatis
personæ of my imagination I knew him as young Orton,
and whiled away some of my hours by constructing
romances about him and the Tichborne inheritance. There
was another man, affectionately known to a circle of
admiring friends as 'Birdie,' who was so like him that it
made me rather angry not to be able to make up my mind
which was the truer claimant. It was, at any rate, something
to do. But 'Birdie' was good-natured also in his way,
though fond of practical joking. I disliked his way of
dipping my hairbrush in the basin in the morning, when I
was too weak to remonstrate, and using it on his own
bullet-head under my eyes; but I bear him no grudge. One
of his amusements did me some harm; for he had a way of
whipping up things in the room and running off with
them—to puzzle me, I suppose, laughing all the time. He
performed this feat once with a new antimacassar; and from
that moment, coupled with the indescribable disorder and
entire absence of all visible supervision over the attendants,
which reigned in the big madhouse, it created in my mind a
notion that there was more dishonesty in the place than
might be. It was a 'delusion,' of course, and the 'notes'
must have had much to say to it; the more as, when it
became known, some of the men would play on it as on an
instrument, as I fear they are but too apt to play in
ignorance, having but too much opportunity so to do, on
the weaknesses and fancies of the poor people in their
charge. The thing is not worth many words, but it is a very
fair instance of the way in which this abominable system
tends to create the very things which it is supposed to cure.
My reflections upon the Orton family—quite as much of a
delusion as the other—are written in no notes but my own.

The warders' faces met mine in the morning; and in a wild opium-trance, acting on the brain at its weakest, I was removed to my prison again. Once during the journey, I learn, I spoke, and once only, when the sight of my colonial indulging in a pot of beer woke the healthy British nature to solicit a drink I do not remember it; for I remember nothing but a confused succession of trains and platforms, till I woke to semi-consciousness in the asylum—to find myself lying on the ground on my back, with a doctor on one side and my old servant—returned from India in the interval—upon the other, contemplating me. This was described as a 'fit'—vaguely. I must have been, like the Yankee of the story, 'a whale at fits,' for I had them of all kinds—epileptic; epileptoid—'toid' meaning nothing, but being substituted when the first 'diagnosis' revealed itself in its native silliness; paralytic (in the left arm, when I had lain on it in bed for some days and rather numbed it); and any others that came handy. I wish I could see those 'notes;' they must be wonderful. But as in the multitude of counsellors is wisdom, in the multitude of maladies is safety. So began my second term—of eight months' imprisonment. Was ever such a story told? There shall be but very little more of it.

VII.

As I look back at the first chapter of this story of mine, and
see that I wrote down that my experience had nothing in it
especially painful, I wonder at the aptitude of human nature
to forget and forgive, where it is only permitted. Now that I
have brought my mind to bear upon the details, they seem
to me fraught with a quite exceptional pain. It needed time
and thought for me to measure, in anything like its depth
and height, the wrong that was done to me. Oblivion alone
shall remain when this my closing chapter is finished; for
forgiveness has in my case been made impossible, since.

Si l'effort est trop grand pour la faiblesse humaine

De pardonner les maux qui nous viennent d'autrui,

Épargne-toi du moins le tourment de la haine:

À défaut du pardon, laisse venir l'oubli!

When I was first imprisoned among madmen, after the
piece of childish folly which had in it no object, if it had
any at all, but to make those come and nurse me whose
clear duty it was to do so, I was so ill and broken that, had
he been in my case,

Mine enemy's dog,

Though he had bit me, should have stood that night

Against my fire.

The second time it was perhaps more cruel still. And the thing was done under cover of the lunacy-laws. If they protect mere heartlessness so, what must they do in cases where purposes directly evil are to be served?

The sadness of this story is affecting me in spite of myself, and makes me anxious to bring it to an end. The second sentence was the same thing over again, except that I knew that I was in an asylum, and resigned myself to feel that I had no chance of escaping. Nobody cared. Why should I escape? I had a few visitors the first time. When they came, a well-set luncheon-table and a good bottle of wine replaced the garbage which we were too often expected to consume, and the unwalled grounds and pretty gardens of Pecksniff Hall were suggestive of a country house in the olden time. My lawyer came to see me and eat mutton—a good fellow, of whom it is pleasant to think, in the bitterness which will mix with my ink as I go on. He happened to bring with him the first copy of the 'World' that I had seen, and left it with me as an odd link with its forgotten godmother. I, with a warder, saw him off by the train, and wondered rather why I should not go too. I had not realised the asylum, and talked to him only of money-matters which had been troubling me. The second time I was too far gone; I wanted no visits, and cared for none, though day after day I woke from my troubled dreams—not all bad now, but some singularly beautiful—with a feeling that surely somebody would rescue me before night. How ill I was after that opium-journey, and whether dying or not, I do not know. The master said that I was, and after the gagging and drugging it is very probable. It was on a hot night in June that I lay down in that evil place again, in the farthest room in a remote wing of the building, between two keepers, who threw themselves one on each side of me, and held me close between them the hot night through, snoring out their own heavy sleep, or waking to hold me closer if I tried to stir. I happened to light afterwards upon the 'notes' of one of them upon this night, in which he reported me as having had some 'bad turns'—of violence, I suppose—in pain as I still was from my fall, and from the gag; opium-dazed and desolate, weaker than a child. For days and nights this went on with a constant change of warders more or less rough and hard. They were told off to watch me three or four at a time, because of my dangerous qualities, and my stupid efforts to get free from them. Among themselves they laughed at it, knowing my weakness; and the smallest boy among them—for there was a stock of small and ugly boys on the staff—would lead me about with his little finger. But sometimes a detachment of them would carry me to my bedroom or keep me down in bed, tearing my clothes in the process. To account for deficiences in my wardrobe (of which each of us had a list, like a schoolboy's) it was said in the 'notes' that I tore them up myself—a 'well-known sign of insanity!' How I dreaded that 'north room'! It was in the oldest corner of the house, cold and hot, and rat-haunted; and much as Mrs. Gamp and her friend must have seemed to their dying-charge, the keepers seemed to me, as they crooned in the corners through my semi-delirium.

It seemed to me that the doctors had wondrous little to say to it. They came to see me now and then, for a minute or two, in my bed. The house doctor, who so impressed my friend, had lived for years in the place, and seemed to have no ideas beyond it. He kept dreadful little things in bottles, and noted conscientiously, by a machine under my window—which looked like the desk of an orchestral conductor—the amount of daily and nightly rainfall. We must all of us do something, I suppose. In the summer he was a great archer, and strutted about with a bow and

quiver. A few of the patients joined in the sport—a
melancholy lord, who never spoke, but was 'my lorded' by
everybody much after the fashion of saner circles, and one
or two others. I tried it once, and was rather gratified to
find that, though I had never used bow and arrow before, I
scored better than the house doctor. But the man-monkey
was allowed to try his hand too, and played hideous tricks
with his arrows, and grimaced so that I could not face the
amusement more. Of the cricket I had enough on my first
visit, and would not run the gauntlet again. To some sort of
distraction I was occasionally driven by despair; for the
constitutionals round the mile-circuit of the grounds, or
among the lanes and roads, were maddening. The Sunday
walks were the worst; when the British villager was out on
holiday, and gaped and wondered at us. In the winter
months I made occasional attempts to follow the pack of
harriers which was kept up for our benefit—which at all
events amused the warders and country-siders a good deal.
I was never fond of harriers, and this was not, perhaps, the
place or time to acquire the taste. Half-an-hour of the
muddy fields tired out the weak body and head, and
aggravated my weary dreams. But it gave a brief space of
comparative freedom; and I was able to associate more
with a good young fellow who came to the place as
companion to the man-monkey, and showed a decided
preference for my society. His berth cannot have been
pleasant; and he found in my room his only refuge from the
general disorder of the house and attendants, though even
there we could not escape from the one tune which one of
them was always beating to death on an ancient piano in
one of the public rooms, to the behoof of the broken nerves
collected there. I had been removed from the north room
then; I suppose in favour of some more violent newcomer. I
found, too, another pleasant companion in an officer who
had seen much foreign service, and liked talk. He wondered

why he was there. He had been ill, he told me. We met first at the billiard-table, and he came up to me at once, and said that he knew my face, and must have met me at Carlsbad, as he had. He was well enough to shrug his shoulders over the matter, and even to find amusement in studying the delusions of the madmen, and talking them over. He had been knocked so much about the world, he said, that he cared little how it all ended; and he had no special desire to meet again the friends who had imprisoned him. I do not wonder. He may have been mad; but I saw him often, and his was the best imitation of sanity I ever saw. At all events it did him small good to be there. We followed the harriers and ate sandwiches together, and speculated why we had been singled out to be crushed by this tower of Siloam. Once, feeling a thought stronger, I wrote a letter to an old literary friend. It was very harmless, for I did not care to complain; but the friend was a member of a well-known legal family, and his name on the envelope caused a sensation. It was believed to be in my officer's handwriting; and he was asked why he had been writing to a lawyer, and what about. Why the heads of an asylum should be afraid of their best friends the lawyers, I do not know. But it seems they are. However, I do not exaggerate. My letter was sent.

The lunatic harriers would make a chapter by themselves; but I have done with them. I began to believe at last that, in the confusion of the whole business, dogs, doctors, keepers, patients, and huntsmen were all going Hamlet's road together. I would give a good deal—prejudice apart—to give some next friends and Head-shakers (the Marcelluses and Bernardos of society—'We could, an if we would—') a few turns with those unearthly hounds. How I passed my evenings, as how I passed my days, save in an occasional study of old novels, an occasional hour at lunatic billiards, an occasional game at draughts or chess with anyone with brains enough to know the moves, I do not know. I was too weak of head and too ill to study, as I have said, or to shake the burrs from off me. On the Sundays I had five o'clock tea with the Master—the only patient so privileged, I think; but he usually talked of one Dr. Blanc and the inferiority of French asylums, failing the elder Grossmith, and I was none the better. Twice did a younger doctor—one of the family and of the firm, for Pecksniff Hall was quite a fact in county society, and had been so for some generations—ask me to dine with him at his house, apart also from the asylum. I found him a good fellow enough, and his wife very kindly; and I despair in conveying to my readers how pleasant it was to dine like a gentleman at a pleasant table. No other patient came; and, as he phrased it, we 'sank the shop.' Did it never occur to him that the 'shop' and I were rather incongruous? He was fond of burlesques, and he was a good hand at billiards; and he looked like a straightforward heavy-cavalry officer. The principal informed me that he received me for the second time against the wishes of his family. I was ill and sentimental, and thought how kind the old man was, and how hard his family must have been to grudge me the only home which I seemed likely to get. I have hoped sometimes since that the family took a view of their own upon the case, and had no wish to make part with mine; but I do not know.

An entertainer, collaborating with a lady-novelist, brought a little play called 'Cups and Saucers' to be enacted in the dining-room. A merry little play, I thought, and the warders and servants liked it well enough. But when I had watched it for a time I retreated to my solitude, for it was more than I could bear. The lunatic next me dilated in a loud voice upon the price of potatoes, which was wide of the plot. He was a wealthy lunatic, and had taken me out for a drive a

few days before, had bared his 'biceps' for my
admiration—it was even less bicipitous than mine—and
waxed very wroth because I asked for his 'Daily
Telegraph,' when he said he had not done with it. Rumours
of war were then in the air; and though it was before the
days when Jingo had become a power, he was more
intensely and demonstratively Jingo than the flower of the
music-halls. If the Home Secretary has profited at all by the
vials of scorn poured upon his head by Mr. Forbes, in his
spirited 'Fiasco of Cyprus,' he must have enough to do just
now in learning the geography of Persia and the Euphrates
Valley; but he might yet find the time to do that imprisoned
Jingo a good turn. Where is the Conservative watchfulness
that leaves such a vote as this to be lost to humanity? There
came a conjuror with a Greek name, whom I avoided; there
came a child-harpist, with a concert, called little Ada
Somebody, whom I would not go and hear; and there were
various parties on the 'ladies' side,' which I could not bring
myself to face.

That ladies' side had for me all the odd fascination of the
unknown. It occupied half the large house; and there was a
little colony of ladies besides in a pretty little house with a
soft poetic name, in the grounds hard by. The native
gallantry of the doctors appeared to keep them constantly
on the ladies' side. If ever I asked for one of them, he was
always there, and would see me when he came back. My
friend the officer penetrated the mysteries, and described
the little card-parties and musical evenings as something
very strange. I could not be induced to go, and the record is
lost. But I met the poor women in my daily walks, and
about the grounds, and learned to know many of their lack-
lustre faces. One of them, in a Bath-chair, accosted me
once suddenly in the public road as we crossed, with one of
the worst words in the English language, and sent me dazed

and dreaming 'home.' The female warders accompanied them; smart young women with a setting of earrings, many of them, who might have been contracted for in the gross by Spiers and Pond; who would exchange many a friendly wink and sign with their counterparts of the male side as they passed. From what ranks they are recruited I do not know, and have no special wish to ask. The sadness of the thing was very deep; for, knowing what we men bore, I speculated much what these caged women might have to bear. The law for us is the law for them. The nervous maladies which attack us, attack tenfold their more delicate organisation; and they are no safer from wrong or selfishness than we. How many times over, to name one danger alone, may the fancies of puerperal fever be miscalled madness, and treated—in these places and among these companions—so? Our wives and our sisters are not very safe from the Bastille, as things now are.

My time went on. During the bitter winter months the asylum was in the hands of workmen, under repair. The great echoing corridors were being papered and painted, the rooms renewed, the chapel decorated in the approved fashion. The workmen were at work by night as well as by day; and the patients slunk about the passages in greatcoats, and warmed themselves at casual fires. I thought that a better time might have been chosen, perhaps; and the confusion seemed to me worse confounded; but that is no affair of mine. 'Would God it were night!' I thought in the morning; and 'Would God it were morning!' at night— when the warders returned with a rush from their hour out, filled the passages with talk and noise and oaths, and with much ceremony brought bed-candles at ten. The plate was beautiful; and some of the candlesticks so big that I used sometimes to wonder whether my keeper for the nonce— they were told off to different rooms every night, to prevent

us from growing too dependent upon anybody, I suppose—
was going to precede me backwards to my bedroom. The
common breakfast began at eight, and the common dinner
was at one. There were two or three different mess tables
for those who lived in common; and the rest ate apart, each
in his own room. For a long time I used the last privilege;
but I gathered at length a sort of desperate courage, and
thought it better to face my kind as much as I could.
Besides, at the common table there was, on the whole,
enough to eat; while the private meals I found singularly
Barmecidal and scraggy. I suppose that, like Oliver Twist, I
might have asked for more. But I was afraid of everything
and everybody, and, fearing a similar result, refrained. The
faces at the board changed little; for ours was practically a
place for incurables. Kindly Death changed them
sometimes, as I have said. Some of those whom I
remembered during my first period had changed visibly for
the worse, like the poor singer of the beer-song, who
seemed to me always struggling with a sense of wrong,
which he could not speak. In the public asylums, I am told,
cures are many. They were not so with us. There were
times when patients were removed to some other asylum—
for the worse, it may be; for I have said that Pecksniff Hall
has the best of testimonials from the Commissioners; but,
with the exception of the friend of whom I wrote, I
remember no case of liberation but one. There was a
clergyman confined among us, whose wife took lodgings in
the village by. She was with him every day, watched him
every day, walked with him every day, and never seemed to
me to leave him till she took him away. Brave little woman,
how I honoured her! for her nerve must have been tried
enough. If these papers of mine make one relation think, as
much as I can hope to do will have been done. The Master
claimed much credit with me for this cure. May he deserve
it! for he must need something to write upon the credit side.

The Commissioners I saw once during my second confinement. They came down, like a wolf on the fold, unexpected. Their approach is, I believe, always concealed from the patients, for fear of upsetting their minds. They came with return-tickets from town, good for one day. They made a sudden incursion into my room—two or three, I forget which, but one was a short lame gentleman who asked questions: Was I comfortable? Had I headaches?— (well, I had that day, from the paint)—and did I hear voices? My chair-covers were being removed at the time, and I had no space to think, much less speak. Twice in the day afterwards I begged of the warders to be allowed to see them again, but neither them nor doctor of course did I see. I say that I was never mad; and there is not an honest reader of this story who will not believe me. And that is all I saw of her Majesty's Commissioners in Lunacy. Was I wrong in calling this a farce? I have nothing to suggest to them. Where work is ill done, criticism may do good. Where it is not done at all, criticism is silent. 'Où il n'y a rien, le roi perd ses droits.' I wrote afterwards, when I was free, to one of them, who had been once a friend of my own, as I thought it my duty to write. He was then functus officio certainly, and well out of it. But he never answered my letter; which I have no doubt he put complacently by, as a madman's nonsense. It must be a comfortable berth enough where officers and doctors and lawyers and relatives are all in a tale, and, in the world below here, there are few to find you out.

As the man to whom I was now to owe my freedom said, this must soon have led to softening of the brain. The strain had become terrible. The belief in the existence of a system of organised pillage among this undisciplined crew, which might well have possessed a stronger head than mine was then, was wearing me out, though I tried to argue myself out of it. Some of the men played on it, as I said. And I was becoming too thoroughly ill and nerveless under this trial to be much more than a sort of automaton. I even began to have a sort of feeling that this was my home, and that I might be turned out to wander again when they grew tired of me. When the relation of whom I have spoken came to stay in a neighbouring town—not at the asylum, happily for me—I was allowed to spend the day like a boy with an exeat, and even in my illness resented the house-doctor's objections to giving me too much leave from school. Conscious of fair powers of heart and brain, the paltry unworthiness of the whole thing jarred me even more than greater sins; and it does so still. How ill I was may be judged from the fact that I did not press, scarcely even wish, for my removal. But the skilful doctor who came to see me—I have reached nearly the last in my story now— who had rescued others besides me, practically insisted upon it; and one morning I received at the asylum the news that I was to go. I could not believe it—could not take it in; thought myself permanently 'on the establishment.' The doctors grinned sardonic disgust; intimated that a serious danger was threatening society, and hinted an au revoir. So did the warders, smiling generally, and holding out expectant hands. I had been allowed a little pocket-money when I was good, but had not much to give. I have not been inclined, upon reflection, to be lavish of donations since. The last report of the 'attendants' was—whether in connexion with this tightness of my purse-strings or not I cannot say—that they had never seen me worse. So the 'treatment' had done me no good, at all events. My new guardian took me to his house by the sea, and, with his wife and daughter, gave me for a time a real home, and was something more than kind. He had not much assistance. From one near relative abroad he received an abusive

letter; from the Master of Pecksniff Hall an angry warning
that he was taking into his house 'a suicidal and homicidal
patient, the most dangerous in his establishment.' But a few
days before the man had made me his guest at his own tea-
table, alone with his wife and young daughters. How does
he reconcile the two things? The charge was cruel, and
nearly robbed me of the hard-won home. My rescuer
believed no word of it; but his wife was naturally
frightened, and for a night or two a new watcher slept at my
door, and I had to submit to a new cross-examination from
two more doctors for the edification of the Commission.
They said that my eye wandered, and drew up such a
certificate that I, who saw it, succeeded in having it sent
back to them. Without seeing me again, they mildly drew
up another in quite different terms, which must be the last
document recorded and docketed in my case. But my sanity
now vindicated itself, and I was free, in spite of the protest
which, by the side of the valuable opinion of the warders,
robs Pecksniff Hall of all title to my 'cure.'

I had still much to bear. For a long time, as I have said, I
was represented as under 'delusions' about my relatives.
The fact that they put me in an asylum, I presume, is
scarcely one. Circumstances were as much against me as
ever, and light-headedness would still threaten to recur,
while asylum-dreams, of course, haunted me still more.
They have left me at last; but I had to fight them down, and
did this time—in Whose strength I have ventured, as I am
bound, to say. I travelled again, and grew better, forcing
myself to new interest in the scenes and people about me.
At last, and in a happy hour for me, I married; though I had
almost made up my mind that I never could. One relative
wrote me an impertinent letter about this 'extraordinary
step;' which is, as the young lady says in the comedy, 'a
thing of frequent occurrence in the metropolis.' Another

wrote to me within a week of my marriage to threaten me with the possibility of being shut up again. It frightened my young wife for some time, she has told me since; but she is a brave woman, and held her tongue. I next found myself charged with 'intemperate habits'—about as near the mark as forgery; and the silliness took away the sting. But it was not nice. It is better to atone for wrong than to excuse it by worse, I think; but it is a matter of taste.

'Liberavi animam meam.' My tale is told, as it was my clear duty to tell it, at the cost of some pain. Let those whose duty it is to mend this wickedness do theirs, or at their peril leave it undone. 'Mr. Hardress Cregan,' says Miles, in the 'Colleen Bawn,' 'I make you the present of the contempt of a rogue.' And, with infinite disgust and scorn, and small hope of better things, I dedicate this true story of the Bastilles of merrie England to all whom it may concern.

'L'ENVOI.'

If the readers of this true history will imagine for themselves a number of hospitals for typhus fever, where any one of them, man or woman, may be shut up among the worst cases upon the first symptoms of a cold in the head—with moral, social, and physical consequences beyond man's power of description—they will know something of the meaning of private lunatic asylums, and our 'lunacy-law.' If they will further reflect upon the chances which they would then have of escaping the infection, they will not wonder that private lunatic asylums are not famous for cures. The matter concerns them more than it does me; for forewarned is forearmed, and I am not afraid of falling into the trap again. But I am not going to shrink, on any comfortable theory of 'letting things alone,' of 'bygones being bygones,' &c., from setting down what I think and what I know. I will be of some help to others if I can. If everybody thumb-twiddled under injuries we should not advance much. I need not to apologise for the directly personal character of the account which I have written; for it is only as a directly personal account that it can be of any value. The imputation of insanity will not trouble me much longer. To those who know me, it is absurd; with those who do not, or who, knowing me, care to repeat it, I am in nowise concerned. If I write this short postscript at all, it is because I have heard, to my great amusement, that since the publication of this history some of my critics have done me the honour to speak of it as in itself a proof of insanity! I can only say with Theodore Hook, if it was he who said it—'Sir, if you can believe that, you'll believe anything.' But they do not believe it. It is the old question of honesty and dishonesty, and concerns me not. I suppose that I am either mad not to hold my tongue, or mad to think they can believe me—anything for a sneer, from time immemorial the safety-valve of dulness or of ill-nature. It is difficult for anyone to believe in such wanton wrong. That is the defence of those who, without the shadow of excuse, have branded me with the most cruel brand that can be stamped on any man. The thing was done. Magna est veritas, in the end: though I think it is growing much more uncommon.

The remedy for having been shut up in an asylum, as a nuisance, is an action for false imprisonment. Thank you. Going to law in England is neither more or less than an amusement for a rich man, who may like to have all his corns hurt, or for a 'company,' who are cornless. You must be prepared to submit to many varieties of insult, with contempt of court if you resent them. I have been a lawyer myself, and of the value of the Law's methods, cross-examination included, as a guide to truth and as a means to justice, I hold my own opinion. I did consult a solicitor, with a view to an action; but from him learned that the first step required of me would be to prove exactly how the thing was done, and exactly who did it, when the whole essence of the wrong was that I was too weak from a common illness to know of what was being done. (If I had been well and strong, I should at least have tried to knock everybody down.) If I made a mistake, I should be 'nonsuited,' or otherwise time-honouredly swindled of my rights: so being sane and having been a lawyer, I let it alone; and was fain to console myself as best I might with Bumble's forcible apothegm—never so forcible as in this case—'The law's a hass.'

The whole confusion worse confounded, which surrounds everything concerning the most palpable, if the most terrible, form of human sickness, had its origin, probably, in the anxiety of kind-hearted people to evade the law of capital punishment on any pretext whatsoever. They called people 'mad' to save them from being hung, when they knew them to be nothing of the kind. Many a sound conscience has been driven into evasion or falsehood as a lesser sin, or a nobler right, than 'abiding' evil laws. This particular form of evasion having been established for good, the Law was prompt enough to take advantage of it for ill, to introduce fresh wrong. For the rest, let my story speak for itself. I have not concealed in any way the extent of the nervous illness into which I fell, aggravated tenfold by this unutterable cruelty. I repeat that it is the most cruel thing that can be done to a nervous sufferer: and it is, or may be, done every day by the Law, which scarcely knows, I think, a wrong it does not favour. This is like finding a man on the brink of a precipice, and, instead of holding him back, giving him a friendly push, with a 'Go over and be damned to you!' The Law will not move in the matter; but for her own honour Medicine may; and I am glad to see that the 'Lancet' has taken the cancer well in hand. I believe that the knell of private asylums will soon be knolled. As soon as we find a Home Secretary honest and brave enough to take the question unflinchingly up, the whole tissue of humbug and deceit will melt like wax in the fire. Amen. For it is time.

He brought me also out of the horrible pit, out of the mire and clay: and set my feet upon the rock, and ordered my goings.—Ps. xl. 2.

Footnote:

[1] This episode is slightly corrected from the account as published in the newspaper in which it first appeared. I had understood that the partnership was between the asylum-proprietor and one of the doctors, in which I was wrong. The correction reads to me like Midshipman Easy's famous apology.

Printed in Great Britain
by Amazon